One
Manchester
Family

ISBN 978-1-54396-492-9 eBook 978-1-54396-493-6

This book is dedicated to my father,

Richard J. Joyal,

soldier, doctor and member of the Greatest Generation. (1915-2006)

"I live on the sunrise side of the mountain"

Brett Kavanaugh, Associate Justice,
US Supreme Court

One Manchester Family

MONICA JOYAL

PROLOGUE

Had it been only months since Meghan MacNamara O'Reilly had made this same trip? Here she was heading back to New Hampshire, but with different plans. The summer on Pawtuckaway Lake had involved much cleaning and clearing around her late father Jack's camp. She had joined the community and reconnected with some old acquaintances, some who were becoming much more than just friends. But more than that, Meghan had become very attached to the place. It had begun to reveal things about her family that she had not known.

Her mother and father retired here and enjoyed years of lake community. After her mother's death, Jack remained active and socially involved in the local town of Hampton Hills and had left much of himself behind in this fishing lodge of his. Meghan was still sorting and discovering. Fall would bring her inside where there were closets, trunks, and loaded bookshelves yet to arrange and sort. And more.

Her brother Ted, who now lived in England, totally surprised Meghan when he informed her that their mother, Sally, had entrusted him with a box. Their mother's only instruction to him was that it should be given to Meghan if she returned to New Hampshire and became interested in the history of the MacNamara family. Meghan had already found Sally's diary. Just as she was packing to return to Arizona and was digging through a chest of drawers, the thick volume had fallen from a woolen sweater where it had been wrapped. Once in Arizona, Meghan found herself spending evenings poring over the pages and listening to a voice she recognized.

Sally had a story to tell. It was the dreams and hopes of a woman who wanted someone to remember the MacNamara name. She wanted someone to record it. The puzzle to her daughter, Meghan, was why?

Everything left of the family seemed to have been stored at the camp. Meghan was beginning to realize that Jack was a bit of a pack rat, but Sally was an amateur historian. Her diary dated back decades. It was choppy and asked as many questions as it answered. How was Meghan supposed to organize such a hodgepodge of entries? Maybe the box from London would help.

The familiar Merrimac River came into sight. Lights shone in homes all over Manchester as the plane circled in to land. The tips of the trees reflected reds and yellow in the late afternoon sun — such a funny season to be going to a camp on a lake. But Meghan felt that she still had an unfinished obligation: to complete the settlement of the MacNamara estate. Sally Hall and Jack MacNamara deserved it, and she would finish the job she'd started on Pawtuckaway Lake. She had a few personal issues to settle as well, so why not remain until she could decide whether she, herself, belonged here?

The next few months would decide. Her own heart would know as well.

CHAPTER 1

Sally Hall

December 1924

Robert Hall stood outside the Sacred Heart Hospital on Hanover Street. He struggled to stop the tears that burned in his eyes. He needed to compose himself. Brenda Hall, his wife, wasn't accustomed to seeing him crying, and he didn't want to upset her. Ten hours of labor was enough for one woman. Sally had already given him a son, Chuckie, and now they had a daughter too. He took deep breaths to calm himself.

Bob had closed his clothing store the minute he got the call from the hospital. He wanted to be there through it all. But in the day, fathers were not allowed into Delivery. It was all a mystery to him, not how it happened — he found himself smiling about that — but it sure had happened, and he had a daughter!

Bob couldn't get past the severe-looking woman in the starched white uniform and white cotton stockings sitting behind the reception desk.

"Bob Hall, here to see my wife, and newborn daughter," he stated breathlessly to her.

Christmas carols came from somewhere. A small tabletop tree full of tinsel and colored ornaments sparkled in the entry hall. Bob headed down in the direction the nurse had pointed and almost leveled an oncoming Santa Claus.

"Sorry, so sorry . . . but my wife is . . ." Bob mumbled.

The man in red smiled and stepped aside.

Brenda Hall lay asleep covered with snowy white sheets. Another nurse put her finger to her lips as Bob approached the bed. She nodded at Brenda, and approached the anxious father and placed his newborn daughter in his extended arms.

As he gazed into the pink face, she appeared to stare back at him, and then she closed her tiny eyes. He slowly settled into a nearby rocking chair set up in the corner of the room, and very gently began to rock.

"Sally," he said. "Just like Brenda's mother. We decided you'll be named Sally." He kissed the sleeping infant on the forehead.

Snow was piled high on the ledge outside the hospital window. A dark sky just to the west revealed a blackening outline of the Uncanoonuc Mountains. The clock on City Hall read four o'clock. Bob and baby Sally rocked together.

For the rest of her life, Bob would tell this story on Sally's birthday. She had ushered in the first winter storm of 1924. Only Bob could get to the hospital that afternoon, with streets piling high in drifts and squalls making travel impossible. Santa himself had delivered her, the story would go.

As for Sally, every first snow found her outside catching flakes on her tongue. She was born in it, she knew. Snowmen would always need hats and scarves and twigs for arms. Even in her late years with some arthritis in her hands, Sally had to venture out and craft a snowball, tossing it at whatever or whoever was in sight. Her world was white the day Sally Hall was born: white walls, white blankets, white snow.

Bob held her close. The tears began again. He looked over at his sleeping wife, Brenda, whose mother had died within the year.

"Thank you," he whispered.

Looking over at a small manger set up on the table to commemorate the upcoming holiday, he sighed.

"Sally White Hall," he told the sleeping child. "Grandma may never have seen you, but you will have her name." He felt content at the decision.

Bob hummed *Silent Night* as winter howled outside in the Queen City. Santa returned later to check in on his patients and snapped a photo of the sleeping pair before the nurse removed the child to a safer place.

It was this photo Meghan found in October 2014, tucked in the back of Jack's old desk. The back of the photo read:

> "December 14, 1924
> For Sally,
> An Early Christmas gift.
>
> Love,
> Santa"

CHAPTER 2

Jack MacNamara

Livingston Pool 1936

Meghan settled back at the camp quickly. The temperature in October came as a bit of a surprise after the warm days she had enjoyed while in Arizona. But it felt good. She dug into any warm pieces of wool or fleece she found among the collection in her parents' remaining clothes. She found herself borrowing from both her parents' closets.

Her brother's box awaited her at the Hampton Hills Post Office, and it was the first item on her agenda. The package was heavy, and she noticed that it had cost a bundle to mail all the way from the UK. Ted had addressed it:

> "To,
> Meghan MacNamara O'Reilly,
> Investigator, Detective and Family Historian
> 123 Clayton Shores
> Hampton Hills, NH, USA"

"Someone has a sense of humor in England," the woman at the post office teased when Meghan picked it up. She then smiled and helped Meghan carry the large parcel to her truck.

4

And so here Meghan was, sitting on the floor of the camp living area, the box opened and piles of confusing envelopes, loose photos, assorted tickets, old posters, cards, half-filled albums, newspaper clippings, and bent folders surrounding her. She still asked herself, what was she to do with it all? She stood and stretched.

The one constant in life on the lake was Max. He had peed on the deck with excitement when Meghan had pulled up in the red truck. Sam had allowed her to store the vehicle at his repair station during her absence and he had picked her up in it at the airport. The dog had refused to leave her side since then. She wondered if the canine half-expected her father to return. How do you explain long absences or death to a dog? No matter. He was delighted to have her back and had not visited the Finches next door since her return.

The dog whined as darkness crept into the late afternoon. Meghan's eyes wanted to close, but each envelope and folder captured another decade, holiday, family member, or ceremony. It was the work of two other women. So far it seemed that Agnes MacNamara was responsible for most of the contents, but it was Sally who added the accounts of the family in her diary.

By placing Sally's diary and Agnes' journal (found among the contents of the box), Meghan was able to begin to make some sense of it all. Apparently, Agnes had been the photographer in her family, and had written a very incomplete journal that sometimes corresponded to the photos. But much of what the box held meant little to Meghan, even with Sally's extra information. Meghan felt mostly overwhelmed with so much to organize.

"Are you hungry?" she sighed and asked Max.

He sauntered over to the sink area and plopped his furry shape next to the cabinet that stored his food. She fed him and quickly led him out to do his business.

She decided to make a tomato and cheese sandwich on Syrian bread and heat up some chicken soup she had made the day before. But her mind wandered back to the images she had just reviewed, piled up in a heap on the floor.

Walking back to the jumble of pictures, she selected one that really touched her. In it stood a small boy in baggy bathing trunks posing next to a tall lifeguard stand. The words on the back —she was beginning to recognize it as Agnes MacNamara's handwriting — read:

"Livingston Pool 1936
Jack MacNamara
'The Fish'"

Meghan knew this story, and chuckled. Her father loved to tell it, and now she had the actual photo to go along with the tale.

*　*　*

Jack MacNamara loved water. And it may be true that sometimes it is easy to confuse dreams or stories we've been told with our own memories, but Jack remembered this incident himself. Agnes claimed that her son could actually smell water. If there was a lake, pond, fountain, or pool nearby, Jack was a human douser. He knew its presence sight unseen.

The MacNamaras grew up in the north side of Manchester near Dorr's Pond. In winter, Agnes brought her sons to ice skate there often. It contained a hut with a center fireplace, an image imprinted in Jack's mind long after the structure had been knocked down and replaced.

One day, Jack wandered off leaving Agnes beside herself with worry. She had been outside hanging laundry when she noticed that he was missing. The swing set was empty. She called Wil when after an hour there was no sign of Jack. They scoured the area. How far could a six-year-old go on his own? As a last resort, they headed toward the pond. They spotted the small boy standing knee deep in mud. He had a frog in a jar and appeared totally unaware of the distress he had caused. It was not the last time he would be drawn there. Finally, Sally took him to the YMCA and signed him up for swimming lessons. He was the smallest in his class, and the instructor felt that he was really too young to be in with the others. But the instructor was soon convinced that only with lessons could Sally safeguard her son and her own peace of mind.

The distance from Dorr's Pond to Livingston Pool was a very short walk. If Wil MacNamara had a dollar for every time his son swam the length of the pool, he could have sent Jack to private school. After the Y, Jack passed all the summer Red Cross swimming classes allowed for his age. He could swim all day and still ask to be taken back in the evening. Jumping from the wall was another thing. There were rules about who could or could not jump.

The original shape of Livingston Pool was more like a liver. There was a diving board, and the entire wall was open to diving. Ladders at both ends made it easy for weaker swimmers to get to them easily, but if you wanted to be able to dive or jump off of the board and the wall, the rule was that a lifeguard had to see you swim the entire length, the long way. Jack, still in elementary school, had to do this.

And so it went that poor Agnes watched in fear as her little Jack approached the very athletic and tanned lifeguard to request such an undertaking. The young man nodded and climbed up on his chair to supervise. The small form of Jack walked to the opposite side of the pool, waded in, and proceeded to swim. For a boy of about fifteen and small for his age, this pool was lake-size. The swim took about five minutes. Agnes just about reached the lifeguard stand when the guard stood up and gave her son the thumbs up sign. He had crossed.

"He's only just turned fifteen," she told the guard. "How could you just let him?"

Apparently, the guard sat down, stared kindly at the panic-stricken woman before him, and smiled.

"Mam," he began, "I've watched your son swim here for years. He is a natural. I bet he could swim the length four times if he wanted to. I just have to watch him do it once."

Agnes, always accompanied by her camera, slipped back to her seat on the other side of the pool. She turned to watch her youngest walk proudly over to the guard where some exchange was made. He then practically ran to the wall and did a seamless dive-off, as if he had been doing it from birth.

He was part fish, his brothers would always claim. And among the many years of MacNamara achievements, this one was captured for all to see. Meghan held the image right in her hands. Agnes had captured it in time.

CHAPTER 3

Pickerel

About 1924

Max lounged at the edge of the deck as if soaking up the remains of the summer heat. Meghan could see orange and red leaves floating out on the deep purple surface of Pawtuckaway Lake. Steam rose from the cup of hazelnut coffee that sat on the table in front of her. Sitting cozily in her fleece vest and sweats, she half-focused on the sepia photo she held in her left hand. The other half of her brain kept glancing out on the lake surface hoping Ed Shea's familiar yellow kayak would appear. She'd been back almost twelve days and he hadn't yet called.

The photo before her had been discovered only that morning from a rather beaten envelope labeled, "Jack." From the size of him, the photo must have been taken when he was around three. The back had been scribbled on with only the word: "Pickerel." It was hard to know who had written the note on this one.

Most of her time since returning from Arizona had been spent winterizing the camp on the inside. She'd put flannel sheets on the beds, dragged out her mother Sally's old quilts, Jack's oversized woolen sweaters and his barn jackets. The kitchen table was covered with a deep red and brown Indian print tablecloth and a centerpiece with orange and brown gourds. One lonely scarecrow stood guard at the back-porch steps. Twice, she had startled herself thinking it was an actual person.

Her coffee was getting cold, so Meghan headed inside, the picture still in her hand. Suddenly, the phone rang.

"Hello."

"Hi, I'm back!" The familiar voice of Ed Shea boomed over the phone. "So, how was Arizona?"

Meghan dropped the photo and plopped on the nearby couch. "It was great! "

She told him all about the trip and what she'd been up to inside the camp. She wondered how cold it might get in the next few months and told Ed how she had ordered a half a chord of wood. It was so easy to just rattle on with him. Then she remembered the photo and, picking it up off the floor, decided to ask him about it.

"Ed, did Dad ever tell you how his love affair with fishing began?"

On the other end, Meghan could hear Ed's breath as he sighed and sat down. She waited.

"As a matter of fact, he did. Why do you want to know that?" he inquired.

"I've been going through a lot of family stuff and found this one photo of him when he was really small. But the label on the back says, 'Pickerel'. Isn't that odd?"

"It all started in a church," Ed began.

"A *church*!" Meghan chuckled.

"Yeh."

* * *

The old monsignor liked his morning walk in the courtyard of Saint Patrick's Church, but the cold was getting to his knuckles today. Father Gagnon knew he needed to get back inside the rectory, but the winter air felt refreshing compared to the stuffy heat inside. From where he stood, he could hear Sister Bridget answering the front door.

"Monsignor Gagnon is out back; come in." Her brogue was still quite noticeable; he'd always liked the sound of it.

The Catholic priest slipped inside the door to the kitchen just as a young man accompanied by two boys shut the front door and paused inside the entrance.

"Hello, I'm Wil MacNamara, and this is my son, Ted. This," he pointed, "is my youngest, Jack."

"Ah, Wil, come in. Nice to see you. Thanks, for responding so quickly."

Monsignor Gagnon closed the second door to the foyer and ushered the man and boys down a narrow corridor to his office, just past the dining area and kitchen.

"Ted is almost ten, so he would be the one I think could help you," Wil explained.

"Fine. That would be great. That's what I need. We have masses at seven, nine thirty, eleven and then at high noon. If I can train him, he could really be of help during Advent. With all the 7:00 a.m. masses . . ." the old priest's voice faded.

"Sister Maria, at the school, sent Ted home with a note. We discussed it and he is willing to serve as an altar boy," Will added.   He nodded with pride at his son.

"I served at mass when I was young," he continued. "My oldest boy, Mike, helps a lot at home, and of course he is kind of busy with playing ball and all."

Wil avoided the old monsignor's eyes. "But, if you need an extra hand, Ted here will be glad to help." Wil tapped his son on the shoulder affectionately.

Wil MacNamara was a Catholic father. It was considered an honor to serve at masses, help with collections, and assist the priests with weddings, funerals, and baptisms. The priest and the father reminisced about how they had both been altar boys and how it was so important to get to the church on time. As they talked, little Jack wandered off.

It was not uncommon for Wil to get distracted and forget that his smallest charge was not afraid to go off on his own if something interested him. There was an old collie that lived in the rectory along with the priests, and the dog had just come down the front stairs. Jack saw the dog and followed it. Laddie was a familiar sight in the school yard just next door. Everyone knew that the dog was friendly. So off Jack went.

Suddenly, Wil remembered that his son was missing.

"Jack, hey Jack!" Wil called.

No answer.

Wil was not much for hobbies. He was not a member of any civic clubs. But he did enjoy fishing on the shores of the local lake, Massabesic. Many Sunday afternoons, he would take his sons for an afternoon jaunt, lunches packed, poles in hand. Of course, little Jack insisted on going along. Agnes, his mother, got quite a kick out of Jack's resistance to any notion that he was too small or too young to go. It was why he was with his father and brother that day.

Father Gagnon, Wil, and Ted headed down the empty hall they had just come from. They could hear Jack's voice. It didn't take them long to find him standing next to Laddie. Jack stood perfectly still, mesmerized by a large fish tank the priests had in the living room.

As if watching a play being put on for his personal entertainment, the boy didn't move. Wil placed both his hands on the boy's shoulders, and turned back to face the priest.

"He likes fish," Monsignor Gagnon stated, amused.

"He sure does," Wil responded. "And more than that. You know what his first word was after Da Da?"

"What?"

"Pickerel. I swear, Father. It was pickerel."

CHAPTER 4

Baptism by Fire

1924

Ed became scarce again after the phone call. Meghan had just assumed that he would offer to go out for a boat ride, but he didn't. He was so helpful about how her father had shown an interest in fish even as a toddler, she'd half-expected him to offer her more insight into the mass of paraphernalia she was digging through. But days went by, and she continued to add whatever she unearthed in the camp to the folders she filled. On this morning, the envelope under study held many pictures of Sally herself. And the accompanying journal proved informative.

Sally's parents must have collected these, she thought. The backside read "1924" — just after Sally's birth. Sally was being held by two adults, a man and a woman, and a priest could be seen carefully pouring holy water over the infant's head. "Sally White Hall" was printed in careful lettering on the reverse and "Baptism by Fire."

From the narrative in Sally's diary, the baptism was described thus:

* * *

Brenda Hall looked frail, but beaming, as she stood beside the baptismal font, holding baby Sally in her arms. Bob took the infant and headed up the aisle of Saint Patrick's Church. Sally was only weeks old, and the mercury registered a negative eleven outside. Brenda wore a raccoon coat loaned to her by her neighbor who, upon seeing the couple heading out earlier in the day, had apparently run out and placed it on the young mother's shoulders.

Meghan could just make out the sleeve of the fur in the photo.

"Mom always told me that she looked like a bear the day I was baptized," Sally wrote. "It was so warm with a slight smell of mothballs. So nice of her neighbor to offer it."

Young Ted MacNamara stood in the small room behind the altar, fidgeting.

Monsignor Gagnon had called him at the last minute to help perform this sacrament. The couple wanted to have their child baptized as soon as possible. Father Paul, the young curate, had come down with a bad cold and couldn't go, so the old priest had to perform the sacrament himself.

To make matters worse, Ted's mother, Agnes Hall, had promised to make a special cake for her sister's bridal shower. So, little Jack MacNamara was in toe. Wil MacNamara was working overtime that Saturday at the cigar factory. He was doing well having just received a promotion, so he didn't want to be absent from the factory. Certainly, Ted could assist, and little Jack would be just fine sitting in a church pew. A box of Crayola crayons would keep him busy. Mike MacNamara would be by as soon as he could, following basketball practice. The overlap wouldn't be more than twenty minutes, Agnes had assured Ted.

Ted could see his younger brother's Red Sox cap just in the third row, Jack's eyes shadowed by the oversized visor.   The priest signaled to Ted, and the boy followed him close behind. The parents switched sides, and the infant was placed into the awaiting arms of the Godmother. She looked remarkably like the baby's mother. The woman cooed and swayed, humming softly to keep the child quiet. And for the moment the church was still.

"You are this child's other parents," the priest began. "She will turn to you both for example and for a clearer understanding of her faith. Should this child, Sally, need Christian models, will you step forward and help guide her to the light of the spirit?" he asked.

"We will," the godparents answered in unison.

From his position to the left of the monsignor, Ted tried to take in the panoramic view of the church. Jack wasn't in his pew. Ted surveyed the large empty rows in the back. The priest moved, and Ted followed. The infant's long, lacy baptismal dress dragged on the floor and, for a moment, Ted's view was blocked. Just as the godparents stepped forward and Ted was directed to bring over the holy oil, a sound of footsteps echoed on the marble floors of the old church.

After that, the story varies.

Ted claimed that he suddenly saw the red of little Jack's Red Sox hat appear directly opposite the baptismal font.

Mike, who had just come in to take command of little Jack, says that his small brother, Jack, dove past the priest almost knocking the old man over.

Someone remembered the smell of burning, and wondered where it came from.

But Jack had already dipped the flowing lace into the holy water. It had caught on fire from the tiny votives that lined the small area next to the font. Before anyone could direct him away, Jack saw the danger and extinguished the fire. Sally whimpered. Brenda snatched her daughter up and screamed. Mike was at the altar in seconds. Ted stood silently beside the priest.

Apparently, monsignor made the sign of the cross, acknowledging that a serious accident had miraculously been averted by the quick actions of little Jack MacNamara.

The photo showed a small boy in a Red Sox hat standing next to the Halls. Family members commented for years how it was that Jack first met Sally and how he had saved her life.

And so, it made perfect sense that the words on the back of a faded photo would read, "Baptism by fire."

Even at three years old, Jack knew his way around water, and Sally Hall was already in his sights.

CHAPTER 5

Love Lessons

Winter, Late 1920s

Meghan found that Agnes MacNamara had chronicled the early lives of her sons both in pictures and journals. When had her own mother, Sally, begun to take such an interest in telling the family story? She couldn't remember that Sally kept a diary, and most of it began to really take shape well into the 1980s, long after many of these pictures were taken.

It was as if Sally had begun her own resurrection of the story of her husband Jack's family, and then came upon some glitches. Clearly, Jack didn't seem so keen on digging up the family story. He had some mementos hidden among his fishing items and Sally had begun to make it her quest to put it all in order, but she died before completing the project. Her mother had safeguarded much of the material by dispensing it off to Ted; he showed no interest in it. And if Meghan had not returned to New Hampshire, surly the tale of the MacNamaras would have been long ignored. Fall and the quiet of Pawtuckaway Lake were giving Meghan much more to think about than getting the old camp into shape for sale.

Among the items in the box were multiple small notebooks put together by Sally. Numbers corresponded to many of the photos, so with a little extra effort, Meghan could tell the story behind the moment captured by the lens. Jack's mother, Agnes, proved to be an avid photographer, leaving it to Jack's wife, Sally, to complete the journal. It would have been so much easier if Jack MacNamara was alive to help, though. But Meghan had to admit, the two women in Jack's life were spanning generations with their words and photos.

There was no picture for the following journal entry, but Agnes had written about it anyway. Meghan could almost hear Agnes' voice in the words. Here was how the entry read:

*   *   *

"Do I have to?" Mike pleaded.

Little Jack sat eating toast and jam in the kitchen as I put another cup of oatmeal into the meatloaf. Jack looked up as I put both hands into the large bowl to mix in the hamburger, onions and egg.

"Can I help?" Jack offered.

Sometimes I let him mix the loaf. He thought it was the best part, except for eating it. Better than mud pies.

"Not today," I said softly as I ran my hands under the faucet to clean them.

Looking up at my oldest son, I sighed. Some days I wished I had a daughter.

"Yes, you do, Michael Patrick. He can skate with the double runners. Ted will be at Dorr's Pond as well. The Dooleys plan to go up, and Jack can skate with little Devlan."

"But I want to play hockey," Mike pleaded.

"When you father gets back, you can go over to the rink. But for the first hour or so, I need you to stay with Ted and Jack on the pond."

There were days I wondered how I had any power in this house full of men.

Later, I would come to find out that it wasn't just hockey on my son's brain — it was Patricia Hannigan. He knew that she would be there. The cold nights had put a thick layer of ice on the pond and it was the perfect place for the young to meet up.

I sent them down to the cellar to dig out the bag of mittens, hats, woolen socks, and skates. Mike was wearing Wil's skates by now; Wil had no time for such winter fun.

I had an appointment for a haircut and permanent. Imagine such a luxury! With Wil working longer hours and bringing home extra money, we looked forward to more outings together soon. I had just enough time after the meatloaf was cooling to get my hair done. Was it asking too much for some time for myself?

And so, off to a very frozen Dorr's Pond went the MacNamara boys. I came back feeling pretty and updated. Wil arrived early, and we all sat down to dinner. It was then that I realized what my little son Jack was learning on the ice.

"Mike likes to skate behind the island," Jack began.

"I thought I told you to stay with your brothers?" I demanded.

Wil had a mouth full of potatoes and just looked up.

"I did," Mike defended.

"I just went after Dad came. You saw me, right?"

"Yes, Mike stayed until I arrived. Then he went to the rink, "Wil confirmed.

Ted looked up and added nothing. Mike reached for more beans.

The table was quiet.

I waited. What was this code of silence, suddenly? And what was Jack talking about? Even Wil seemed content to let the subject drop. But little Jack wasn't.

"Mike fell over the snowbank at the edge of the pond, I think to save some girl who fell there too," he stated without any emotion.

Again, silence fell over the table.

Wil gave me a look — a look I will never forget, a look that will stay with me forever. Something had shifted among the men, and I was not a part of it.

"Do you think Patty Hannigan is pretty?" Jack grilled his oldest brother.

"Very," was all my son could mutter before excusing himself from the table.

Jack lingered that night. Wil disappeared into the living room and lost himself in the evening news. Ted followed Mike up their bedroom. Only Jack and I were left to dry the dishes.

"Hey, Mom," Jack said. "The Dooley girl sang 'Mikey loves Patty' when we were all skating together. She says they were kissing behind the snowbank. She said that I love Sally, too, because of what I did at the church."

At that moment, I realized that my oldest son was no longer mine. The love of his life had arrived. And little Jack had had his first lesson on love, too. But no one, not even he, knew it then.

CHAPTER 6

Crystal Lake:
The Hermit and Broken Hearts
1927

If the summer on Pawtuckaway Lake proved full of surprises for
Meghan, late summer and early fall delivered even more of the unexpected. She'd already learned much about her father's life in retirement
on her own ventures into Hampton Hills and the lake. But cooler days
spent inside revealed tales and images from before the lake days.

A wet smooch from Max woke Meghan to morning. Sitting beside
the bed, he stared until she opened her eyes.

"Hungry, are we?"

Max was always ready for a meal. She got up, wrapped herself in a
fleece robe, and headed for the porch to let him out. As he munched con-
tentedly on his kibble, she heated water and made herself some Chai tea.
Cooler weather seemed to suit its rich flavor. She'd sampled the tea at the
Finch's and had switched over to it for the fall.

Meghan headed for the porch, wisps of steam rising from her cup.
Fog lifted from the surface of the lake, but no kayak appeared. She missed
those summer morning rendezvous with Ed.

"Where is Ed?' she asked Max.

He tilted his head.

"He can't be *that* busy, can he?"

Bob Finch had come over a few days earlier to help her unload two large pumpkins that she just had to have. They rolled out of the back of the truck into his able arms. It was her opportunity to try at subtlety.

"So, Bob, what's Ed been up to since he returned from California?" she asked innocently.

Bob grunted and lifted the second orange monster.

"Did you have to get the biggest ones they had?" Bob said kiddingly.

He was stalling.

"He's been going through all his years of being principal. He told me that he has boxes piled up in his garage, office, and den. The school dropped off more. He has really retired this time and has years of stuff to sort. You know him; he admits to being a pack rat, like your father. He has time now to really go through it. That's all I know."

Bob knew she felt slightly abandoned, but he left with only a friendly nod.

And that was the extent of her new knowledge. October was just around the corner, summer was waning and Meghan needed to get her mind back into the inside projects of the camp.

"With that in mind," Meghan looked over at the dog, "let's head into Dad's assortment of winter clothing."

Her plan was to empty the old oak, six-drawer chest in Jack's back room. It seemed to have become the catch-all of anything her father couldn't fit inside the smaller bureau. A good cleaning would clear her mind as well as the stuffed drawers.

She was right. She could barely pull the drawers out; they were so jammed up with clothes, mostly old waffle thermal underwear. She remembered borrowing such items as kids when winter nights proved to be too cold for standard pajamas. They made wonderful substitutes.

"I'm going to use some of these this winter," she proclaimed to Max, who had already found a piece of bottoms and lay down on one.

She wondered if Jack's scent remained; a dog's sense of smell was extraordinary. Max curled his large golden body tightly on the small piece of waffle cotton, and drifted off to sleep.

A pile of bottoms and tops began to grow on the floor. Jack had some of what he'd referred to as his "union suits" in red and blue. The behinds on these had open panels that closed with buttons. She had to chuckle. Jack wore these with woolen shirts. As small kids, they used to come up behind him when he was shaving, pull down the back panel and run down the hall giggling and calling, "Daddy, do you feel a draft?"

The collection filled up the lower two drawers in the chest. Underneath, her father had lined the old, cracked drawers with newspapers. Ordinary brown grocery bags had been used to do the job too. She would reline the drawers and wash most of the contents, selecting what was worth keeping. The remainder would go to the church donation bin in town. She might have a time getting Max's selection from him. Maybe he could keep it.

The dates on the yellowed newsprint under the old liners were mostly from the 1980s. Sally had left Jack to do his own thing in this part of the camp. It was obvious that she hadn't ever tried to organize this mess. Some thermals had no tops. Some were stained with what looked like paint. Meghan tore all the old newspapers and rolled them up for trash. Some of the paper stuck to the sides of the drawers, so she dug her fingernails in to detach it from the wooden sides. That was when she discovered a small piece of newspaper folded carefully and hidden inside a coiled envelope. Inside was a wedding announcement dated May 1929. The name of the couple read: "Mr. and Mrs. Craig MacGuire."

Meghan stared at the clipping. She knew this name. Was it an aunt and uncle of Jack's? The name was Irish. The date was important. It was just before the crash.

"Maybe," she thought out loud.

Hadn't Sally related something about that name? Meghan headed for Sally's journal. Within minutes, she had found it. Little Jack must have related more to his mother than he was supposed to, because the story took up three pages in Agnes' diary. His mother put it all together for someone else to read decades later. The tone to this entry was reflective. The style revealed Agnes' writing abilities. It was as if she had begun a chapter of the MacNamaras' book, the one no one had yet been able to finish. Meghan placed the announcement next to the corresponding words written in Agnes's now-familiar script. She reread the entry:

* * *

Jack MacNamara watched his big brother Mike stare at himself in the hall mirror routinely. Mike combed and recombed his unruly hair, brushed his teeth shiny and readjusted the grey cap he'd taken to wearing. His toothbrush lay wet on the bathroom sink; steam covered the mirror. Mike sure wanted to look good and smell right. Jack kept opening the window after Mike left, but Jack wasn't complaining. A date with Patty Hannigan meant Jack might be taken along.

Over the winter, Mike took to asking little Jack if he wanted to go along when he went sledding at the Derryfield Park. Generations of residents of Manchester grew up riding the small hill on the side of Mammoth Road. Wil worked so hard these days, even Saturday had become a full work day. So trips to the snowy hill had become a routine with Mike letting Jack sit on the sled when it was being pulled back up the hill. This must impress the ladies, Jack figured, the most important of whom was Patty Hannigan.

Jack got to ride with Mike and Patty on her toboggan. She screamed in his ear as Mike tore left and right, cutting off oncoming sleds. And Jack learned never again to mention anything about Mike's girlfriend to his mother.

By the time summer arrived, Mike and Patty had been doing a lot of handholding. Jack often accompanied them over to Crystal Lake to swim. He learned a lot about the lake during these excursions. Mike liked to show off his knowledge to Patty. Years later, Jack would relate these stories to his own children, and Meghan and Ted knew most of them.

Crystal Lake consisted of a bathhouse and picnic area. During the 1920s, the city of Manchester sponsored swim meets for children there. Jack participated; Mike had the perfect excuse to invite Patty, and to register his brother, Jack, in these contests. Then they all could stay at the pond for hours. Jack's love of water merely added to the certainly that he would want to accompany the love birds. Mike knew that his little brother Jack was a babe magnet.

"It was here, on what was once called Skenker's Pond, and then Mosquito Pond, that the hermit once lived," Mike began on that hot afternoon in 1927.

Jack would remember that day. Patty and Mike sat on the old beach blanket, the one that was stored perpetually inside the Model T in the heat of 1927.

"Don't you two know about the hermit?"

Mike had them now.

Patty's eyes sparkled. Jack sat mesmerized by the old story.

"What hermit?" Jack inquired.

"Well," Mike began slowly, winking at Patty.

Jack wrapped himself up in Mike's old grey sweatshirt. They all lay back on the blanket and stared up at the ever-forming shapes of white clouds that passed over Crystal Lake. It was so perfect. Jack felt safe. Mike and Patty were in love. All was well in the world of Manchester and the MacNamara boys that warm, summer day.

Mike pushed his hair back, his eyes resting on the woman before him, admiring her. She looked especially shapely in her cobalt blue swimsuit. The story became the background for a day to remember in Jack MacNamara's young life.

"The hermit's name was Charles Alan Lambert. He came in the 1890s to Mosquito Pond. He had been jilted, and to mend his heart, he threw himself into growing and selling herbs."

"What's jilted and what's a *herb*?" Jack remembered asking.

Mike stopped to explain. "He had had his heart broken and came here to recover. An herb — you don't pronounce the 'H' — is like mint or oregano."

"Or pepper," Patty added.

The hermit of Mosquito Pond apparently stayed on the pond for sixty years. He lived in a log cabin he had built, and people came to buy his products. He never married. When he died, he was buried in Saint Joseph's Cemetery. His tombstone reads simply: "The Hermit."

Jack remembered that Mike leaned over and planted a kiss on Patty's mouth. Jack had looked away. Patty blushed and gazed over in the direction of the bath house, as if to distract them.

"The park is really full today," Patty observed. "And isn't that Craig MacGuire over there with all of his buddies?" she had pointed.

Jack and Mike looked over to see a growing crowd of young men in bathing trunks tossing a ball around. Jack noticed something in Patty's eyes he couldn't yet define. But even then, he felt a sense of something foreboding, and he didn't like it.

This clipping meant something. Jack learned about a lonely heart and how love can go. It was the last summer Mike and Patty spent at Crystal Lake together. This was Patty's wedding announcement — to someone else.

*   *   *

Meghan read the rest of the well-flattened clipping she held in her hands:

"On May 11, 1929, John C. Hannigan gave his daughter Patricia Ann Hannigan in holy matrimony to Craig R. MacGuire in a double ring ceremony held at St Patrick's Catholic Church. The bride wore French lace. A reception took place at the bride's home. They will honeymoon [at] Well's Beach, Maine. The groom is a graduate of Manchester High School."

Brother Mike introduced his little charge to love, loss and the hermit at Crystal Lake that summer day. Jack had been there through it all, and here was the proof. Agnes and Jack knew; mother and son would never forget. It was a part of the story of one Manchester family.

Meghan placed the clipping carefully on top of the bureau. She had another piece of her father's life to add, and the tale of a young man's heart to remember.

CHAPTER 7

Ed Returns

2014

lice Finch had dropped by almost every morning with two cups of coffee in tow, staying only minutes, as if looking in on Meghan but not wanting to intrude. Neither mentioned the obvious absence of Ed's yellow kayak. The antique boat belonging to Ed Shea had been seen once at the neighbor's dock, but only once.

Her neighbors also dropped hints about all the goings-on around Hampton Hills over the fall months, an effort to entice Meghan to plan her social calendar. Meghan realized that since returning two weeks ago, she had been consumed with photos, journal entries, and camp winterizing. Alice's invitation to join a local scrapbooking club sounded like a practical solution to organizing the hundreds of pictures Sally had left her. She wasn't much for scrapbooking per se, but it would give her an excuse to get out and solve some of the mystery behind many of those old images. There were still dozens she could not identify.

She and Ed Shea had spent a lot of time together during the late summer. Without realizing it, he had filled much of her time, and now that she was back, she just expected him to be a continued presence. Bob's admission that the man seemed somewhat otherwise occupied had crept into her psyche, and she wondered if it had all been just his way of helping her segue into fall. He was back from California and his family visit. She shook her head and told herself to stop worrying. It was probably nothing.

As if in sync, the phone rang.

"Hi," a friendly male voice said. "Want to go for a pizza? I have nothing in this place to eat!"

Ed was back.

A wide smile broke over her face. "Pizza sounds great! Give me an hour."

The days were already decidedly cooler, but Meghan wasn't ready to wear heavy clothes. She needed to go shopping. It had been easier to simply add layers of clothes from whatever was already in the camp. It occurred to her that maybe old plaid, well-worn flannel shirts weren't the most attractive outfit for a date. When had she decided that these excursions were dates? It was one thing to pull on whatever lay around or had been stuffed into drawers, and another to pull herself together. She knew she could use something new to wear.

She remembered that there were a few shirts still wrapped in cellophane in the bottom of her father's tall chest of drawers. A recent arrival of catalogues had showed many young women wearing plaid shirts over tank tops, sleeves rolled up and shirt tails tucked into the front of jeans. She could easily put together this look. Meghan headed for Jack's room and yanked out the large bottom drawer. The oak squealed. She wiggled it from side to side, and sure enough spotted a tangerine and blue plaid flannel. It was still in plastic. If there was a nice white tee, it would work. Had to love Jack's shirts.

Her father didn't arrange his drawers. He was definitely a stuffer. The packaging must have melted to the inside of the back of the drawer, so a mass of well-worn shirts would have to come out first. The pile on the floor grew.

"Finally!" she sighed as the shirt came loose in her hands.

It seemed that the shirt wrappings had been wedged under a metal photo frame that lay flat against the back corner of the drawer. She loosened it, and held the frame before her. She remembered this one. It had been on their parents' bureau in Connecticut. It was a photo of Jack and his childhood dog, Conway. Jack kept it with pictures of Meghan and her brother Ted. The old image of the dog among the MacNamara photos had gradually become faded and yellowed, surrounded by newer versions of the children as they grew up. But for many years, any family picture included Conway. This particular picture of Conway reflected the stature the pet held as a member of the MacNamara clan. Meghan hadn't seen it in years, but here again was another example of Jack's hidden stash of memorabilia.

She wondered if it had been labeled. She hoped so. Carefully removing the cardboard backing on the frame, Meghan slipped out the photo of Conway. To her delight, in the clear handwriting of Agnes MacNamara, there was a notation on the back:

> "Jack and Conway,
> Massabesic Lake
> June 1930
> FISHIN'"

Some added information on the bottom of the back looked like the words "YELLOW PERCH." This was her father Jack's handwriting.

Sally's diary repeatedly insinuated that, when Jack finally retired to Pawtuckaway Lake, the past was to be left behind. He wanted little that was not lake-related to be moved from the family Connecticut furnishings. And that meant photos. Why else had she shipped them off to Ted in another country for posterity? The same reason she had kept such good records of her own? And here was Jack hiding this framed heirloom. Carefully, Meghan propped it up on the top of the chest. Lost, found, and remembered.

Glancing at the clock, Meghan remembered why she had gone digging around in her father's clothes to begin with. Ed would be by, and she was once again lost in her archeological diggings. She could shower in three minutes; she needed to. Leaving a trail of cardboard collar pieces, torn cellophane, and dropping pins into her empty coffee cup, Meghan stripped off her clothes and headed for the shower.

"Max, I just found a picture of your lost cousin. Did you know you had a dog relative?" she asked the Golden Retriever. "He was Jack's first dog," she added giving Max a light tap on the back.

He followed her to the bathroom and lay down patiently outside. He was getting accustomed to these exchanges and hoped it meant dinner would not be forgotten.

Quickly drying and heading for her room, Meghan pulled on her snuggest jeans, rolled up the cuffs and slipped into flip flops. She had no real shoes to wear. The white tee peeked out from the crisp, orange-blue collar. Gold earrings flattered the new fall shades, and her brass cuffs set it all off. That navy sweater of Sally's fell nicely over her shoulders. She pulled her hair up with a clip, and voila! Good enough.

"Are you hungry?" she inquired, knowing the answer from the immediate wagging and drooling.

"Want dinner?"

She was just cleaning out Max's bowl when a tap could be heard from the screen door. Max galloped over, barking excitedly.

"Hey, old boy. How are you?" Ed's voice greeted the furry figure. Ed leaned down and rubbed Max's ample sides with both hands while the canine placed a wet kiss on his face. Meghan felt the urge to do the same. Well, almost.

He put his arms around Meghan and held her for a moment. She leaned into him and relaxed. He kissed her lightly on the lips and stared at her before stepping back and winking. "So, we are both back. I missed the lake out there in dry California."

Ed watched as Meghan quickly filled Max's dish. Max ate noisily while Meghan chatted to Ed about the changes in the lake with the coming of autumn. He stepped aside as they headed out onto the porch and directed Max to go to the Finches. As soon as they were in Ed's Outback, Ed began to relate the details of his trip to California.

"All my nieces and nephews are enjoying life. My niece, Carol, is pregnant with her third. My cousin, Larry, bought a new car — a hybrid. We celebrated some birthdays, mine included. There was so much to catch up with. That's why I ended up staying for the extra week. It had been so long since I had such a stretch of time. As an educator, it was the first time I actually took a vacation in September! This is such a great time of year to travel."

Ed smiled over at his passenger, realizing that he had not stopped talking since he had picked her up.

"When was your birthday?" Meghan wondered.

"Oh, it is September 17."

Meghan was silent for a minute as she realized that she didn't know this. Was it because they had been avoiding any mention of the age difference? Or was it that they had been spending time doing things together much of the summer and hadn't really gotten into personal information? She didn't know his birthday, and felt remiss.

"I'll make you a belated birthday dinner," she announced.

"I'd like that."

The rest of the evening was the way many had been. They ate companionably and chatted about all the events of the past three weeks. Ed expanded more about his own childhood and about how much reminiscing he found himself doing when he was with his extended family. So many memories and stories were retold during his trip west. Meghan listened, feeling the same way about the emotions she'd been having as she categorized the massive collection Sally had left her. But she wasn't ready to reveal this, yet.

As she sipped her glass of merlot and munched on a pepperoni, Meghan could feel her shoulders drop. Ed Shea had grown up in the same neighborhood in Manchester as the MacNamaras. Their lives had overlapped because Ed hung with Ted. Now he was spending time with her, but she really didn't know him. Perhaps, he could shed some light on the complete MacNamara story, the one Sally seemed to want to be told.

But not tonight. She sat enjoying the warmth of her wine, the company of Ed and the image of Jack and his dog Conway. Past and present met, and it felt very nice to be back on Pawtuckaway Lake.

CHAPTER 8

A Missing Person

1930

Meghan stood on the threshold of the camp door. The early morning air held a chill as if a tease of the coming winter months. She let the smell of minty chamomile tea fill her nostrils. Tea in all its variety was becoming a staple in her morning routine. The steam drifted lazily into the air around her head. She took a deep breath just as Max pushed by chasing something. Nose to the ground, he headed toward the shed behind the camp. Probably just a squirrel, she thought. Wrapped in her robe, she decided to follow him. She pulled a chair out to the sunny side of the camp and sit. Warm summer days were slipping quietly away.

Max's posterior was visible around the north end of the shed. He had followed something, and it was probably hiding behind one of the supporting concrete blocks that the shed sat on.

"Max, just a chipmunk or something. Come," she called to the dog, but he stood his ground, continuing to poke his nose and scratch his paw at the back corner of the small building. He barked, glanced over at her and then back at the spot of interest.

"What?" Meghan asked as she tightened her robe and carried her cup over to where he stood.

Living with Max had taught Meghan to heed his signs. She had come to recognize the difference between his various barks, whimpers, and warnings. It might be that the mail had arrived out on the road, or a passing boat had come in a little too close to the shore. She either shrugged it off as not important or responded by checking it out, just to be sure. Meghan needed no doorbell if visitors showed up at her door.

Max did not come, so she approached him and circled his location, scrutinizing the wooden corner of the shed that held his undivided attention. She knelt and peered behind the block. At first, she could make out nothing but a lot of broken rocks and dry dirt. Max pawed the underside of the shed and whimpered.

Kneeling now, Meghan bent down to angle her head so that she could see the underside of the shed. Sure enough, a hole had been eaten through. Some animal was preparing to make a nest inside for the winter. Bits of wood chips lay in the dirt. She stood and headed around to the front of the small structure to investigate from the inside.

Heading for the back corner, she realized that the hole was hidden from view. One of Jack's workbenches blocked access. She put her empty cup down and, with both hands, attempted to pull the old oak table away from the wall. It wouldn't budge. She began to move the heavy tools to the bench on the other side of the shed. If one critter was inside, it was a welcome mat for more and bigger animals to follow. She should take care of it while the opening was still small.

This was really not a job to be doing still in her pajamas and robe. But like her canine friend, she had started something and was determined to finish it. Her curiosity piqued, she had to check out the damage and decide the culprit. It was most likely a field mouse, chipmunk, or red squirrel, preparing nests for the oncoming cold.

With most of the heavy tools removed and the old vice reinstalled on another table edge, Meghan braced herself. Placing both hands on the edges of the workbench, she used all her weight to wiggle the table loose and yanked using all of her weight. Her hands slipped. She grabbed the knob on the drawer for a better grip, but tripped over the belt of her now-untied robe and then down she went falling back onto the floor. The contents of the drawer spilled all over and around her.

"Great!" she yelled.

Max hovered over her and placed a wet kiss on her upturned face.

Apparently, the drawer contained most of Jack's miniature tools. Small screwdrivers, pliers, and tiny pointed instruments of all kinds were strewn around her head. She had to laugh.

"I could have done without this mess!" she mocked herself.

Getting to her feet, Meghan began to replace the multiple small tools back inside the drawer. She headed for the empty drawer, pulling it to herself, and reached for a tool. Before dropping it inside, she found three sets of eyes staring up from the bottom of the drawer.

Hidden from view, lying flat on the bottom, was a duplicate photo of the one taken at Massabesic Lake. But this one must have been taken minutes later, and depicted not only Jack and Conway, but a man who looked remarkably like Jack — Wil MacNamara. It was the rare photo of Jack's dad. There was only a date on the back: "1930."

Other than Agnes, the one person who was the least photographed among all the photos that Meghan had viewed to date was Wil. She knew only that Jack's father had died young. Jack kept this moment captured in two places at the camp. What was more important to Jack than his dog, fishing, and the father who taught him how? How many other items had Jack kept from them? Again, the evidence didn't gel with Jack's position to leave the past behind. In his own way, Jack too had kept a trail of family facts. But you had to stumble onto them.

Nightly, Meghan had been reading Agnes MacNamara's journal. She would stop and refer to her mother Sally's diary for hints about the possible time, year, or events reflected in the image. This particular day at the lake had been photographed twice, and oddly, Jack had both copies. So he wanted to live in the present, except when it came to some things. And this one memory apparently was one of them; he wanted to preserve this image.

She replaced all the tools, worked the drawer back into the bench, dusted herself off, and headed back inside the camp. The invaders would have to wait. Mice would winter here as they had for years. The scat she saw looked to belonged to them. Max chased red squirrels up the tree, the odd grey squirrel as well. There was a lot of life housed in Jack's old shed. But repeatedly, the life she found was his own. Meghan wanted more information on both the circumstances of this photo and the faces looking back at her. Meghan hoped she would find answers in the words of Sally's recordings or in the other photos of Agnes' collection.

Jack was proving to be more sensitive about his family than she had ever suspected. The camp clearly did hold the heart of Jack MacNamara, and Meghan felt more determined to put all the various parts together.

CHAPTER 9

Conway

Winter 1932

Sally's diary and the beat-up journal of Agnes MacNamara were marked with yellow, pink and green post-its. Somewhere in there Meghan knew there were answers to the entire collection; they were just being revealed at a snail's pace. The pile of unmarked photos had begun to grow, and she was now subdividing them into faces and places that looked familiar. Jack's dog had shown up in one of Agnes' earlier entries. If only Meghan could find it.

It took some digging. Meghan didn't want to mark over the handwriting of the ladies, so she placed her post-its carefully. Some fell out. She seemed to remember that Agnes had done one of her longer writings on Jack's dog. She needed to find it. And finally, she did. And like an omniscient writer, recording the story unfolding before her, Agnes related the story of the MacNamara's dog herself. Meghan could put picture to truth. Agnes told it herself as a spectator in her own life. Parts of the MacNamara family were so disjointed and often misleading at times. This narrative by Agnes reminded Meghan that her project did have teeth. She just had to stay with it. The pieces of the puzzle fit perfectly this time.

* * *

Conway's Arrival, Winter of '32

Agnes MacNamara's hands dug elbow-deep into the hot dishwashing water. The heat rose, steaming up the window before her. Her stomach was soaked through the cotton apron she wore. In the glass, reflected in the window, she could make out herself and the image of her eleven- year-old son, Jack. He continued jumping in the snow piled high against the yard wall. He was playing with a dog. Four weeks had passed, and still the canine remained. It had in fact not left the boy's side since arriving.

They woke up one cold Monday to odd squealing coming from the front porch. Jack had been up as usual, earlier than the rest, and followed the sound only to discover an old blanket full of puppies. Of the original three, two never survived the night, but this one dog refused to lose the battle. Wil let Jack sleep with it on the living room floor. Agnes swore her son's determination, plus the pup's will to live, saved its frozen body.

"Conway" was the named given to it. Jack named it after Passaconaway, the great chief of the local Abanaki tribe. Ted had told his younger brother stories about this local Indian on recent fishing trips to Massabesic Lake. Legend had it that the figure was to have disappeared, just the way this small animal appeared, in bad weather.

"Passaconaway paddled in a canoe near Loon Island when a storm came up. He and his vessel vanished, possibly hit by lightning," Ted had related to his impressive charge.

The story stuck to the boy's imagination, and naturally, the dog received the blessing of the name. The name was abbreviated to Conway, and the dog joined to the archives of a boy's childhood, one filled with adventures and myths.

All Wil MacNamara would admit to was what he had always said of pets: "Once you name something, it's yours." He may have also mentioned that the last thing they needed was another mouth to feed.

But Jack missed his older brother Mike, who was gone most days in search of work. Mike took the train daily to Boston, knocking on doors and returning empty-handed. Wil's work was sporadic at best. Economic rough times hit the Queen City as hard as it had hit any other mill town in America, with a dark cloud hanging over all. Conway was at least a comical distraction.

Agnes studied her hands, raw and cracked by the harsh lye in the soap. She had begun to take in laundry to make ends meet. The fancy hand cremes she used to apply were long exhausted. Butter rubbed on periodically helped relieve the worst of it.

She watched Jack toss snowballs into the air. The antics of Conway's chasing and retrieving made her smile slightly. All around her their small world seemed unsure, afraid, and shrinking. Two neighbors had foreclosed only the year before. Houses stood empty.

Jack and Conway had disappeared around the back street, but reappeared eager to report something to Agnes.

Cold air brushed against Agnes' bare legs as boy and dog rushed in. The brown canine sat at her feet as if sensing the power she had over its fate. Agnes moved away from the warm furry thing, trying not to show her amusement.

"Wipe your feet, and that dog!" she chided. "And close the door."

Jack rummaged under the kitchen sink to retrieve an old rag. Stepping carefully from ice-clad boots, he unbuckled the metal hinges and stepped carefully onto the rug in rag-wool feet. He lifted each of Conway's paws and wiped them dry before standing directly before his mother.

"Mom, when Conway and I were out in the back, a man stopped us. He wasn't looking for food, or anything from me. I know I'm not supposed to talk to strangers, but he really seemed to want to pet Conway. And we got to talking, and well, he asked me how old I was. I look older.

Everyone thinks I am since I grew, and so I said I was thirteen. And so well, he thought that that was a good age and a responsible one."

Jack's eyes never left the dog's face.

"So, anyway, he asked if I would go over and shovel his sidewalk. He lives only four blocks away, and he has trouble with his back. He'll pay me if I promise to do it all winter. I said that I'd have to ask. Can I?"

He finally stared straight into his mother's face and waited.

"We sure could use some extra money. Did he say how much, hon?" She dried her hands and looked off into the deep snow beyond the kitchen window, absently dipping her left index finger into the plate of butter to smear some on her hands as she considered this.

"Ten dollars for five storms," Jack announced proudly. "It can pay for Conway, too. He eats a lot."

Years later Agnes would relate this moment. It was a well-told family story. She would claim that that dog was worth his weight in gold and therefore his breed was Golden Retriever. To her that was what he was if anyone really needed to know.

Conway lived to be about sixteen. He saw Jack into manhood. One winter day Conway came in after a walk in the snow and fell asleep near the front door. He never woke up. It broke Agnes' heart.

*　*　*

Meghan marked the page. Again, she had uncovered more of the MacNamara story. Agnes would have been pleased that someone was reading her recordings. Sally had left enough crumbs for Meghan to follow the trail. And just when Meghan felt lost, a nugget like this one showed up. She had both photographs of Conway together now. And like relatives separated at birth, members of the family seemed to be finding one another amidst the bits and pieces of saved pictures, and a mother's words.

CHAPTER 10

Last Victory

1928

E d Shea promised himself that when he returned to Pawtuckaway the first thing on his list would be to clean out years of accumulations in his camp. He was retired, had had a great three weeks away on the west coast and now that he was really retired, he needed to clean out the old. And so here he sat at his kitchen table overlooking an early fall lake, holding one of many photographs he had found. He sipped a cold beer. In the early evening light, his eyes could melt into the memories he held. Truly a picture is worth a million words, and if some of these photos could talk, they would tell a tale.

But as he was beginning to realize, these photographs didn't just represent his life with Joanne, but the stories of those families whose lives crossed paths with his. The most prominent were the memories shared with the MacNamaras.

Meghan had been so sweet to invite him to celebrate his birthday, even if it was over a week ago. In the course of their recent pizza outing, she had mentioned that the project she was really getting into this fall was the organization of the MacNamara collection of family history. She had pictures, journals, diaries, and assorted newspaper clippings, along with all the rest of the paraphernalia that Jack had just stored wherever. Meghan's mother, Sally, had left more records in England, based on Ted's recent letter, as well.

What was troubling Ed was not what to give Meghan to add to her genealogical investigations, but what to keep from her. How much did she already know about Jack's lineage? The 1930s had disrupted the country; the MacNamara clan had not escaped unscathed.

The particular one that had his attention, however, was a very yellowed one that had slipped from an old album belonging to his own father, Sean. Joanne had also taken to sorting and organizing their collection over the winter months they'd lived on Pawtuckaway, and she had learned a lot about the Sheas in the process.

Joanne called relatives asking questions. She purchased scrapbooking materials and utilized colorful paper and edging to create attractive albums. His daughter Kate was especially happy when she received one as a Christmas gift for her son, Dan. The small boy would never recall any of these people, and Ed liked the idea of such a memento. Recently Ed had found more loose photos in a box in the bottom of Joanne's closet. The box contained images that she had not recognized at all. He, however, did.

The latter collection was of times before he and Joanne even knew one another. They were of his days playing basketball with Ted MacNamara. Here among the twenty young faces staring back were bookends of two young coaches: Wil MacNamara and Sean Shea. Both Ed and Ted had been on their fathers' basketball teams at Saint Joe's High School in Manchester.

The memory caught in his throat. So much lay ahead. At the time of this team photo, Wil and Sean were men in their prime with the world ahead of them both. The next year would tear at the very fabric of Manchester and the country. Alcohol filled the gap for many fathers. Sons felt their fathers disappear from their lives, many becoming hollow versions of their younger selves.

In the old picture, Wil held a trophy high above his head, smiling the smile of the victorious. His arm surrounded Ted's shoulder. Sean Michael Shea was half on one knee next to Ed at the other end of the bench. He too held his head high in pride, leaning into his son.

Sean Shea had kept a silver-framed edition of this very image on his work desk. It marked the entrance of his son from grammar school into high school competition. Within months, the teams dismantled as men and boys searched the countryside for any way to make a dollar. But not that day.

Wil MacNamara had left on a train like many men, but never returned. Sean contracted a lung infection within a decade and died. Today it would have been treatable probably, but not then. Neither man lived to see the next generation.

So, when Meghan informed Ed about her investigations into the family background, Ed received this news with a mixture of admiration and sadness.

"I am finding that Agnes was a great photographer. And my mother Sally did really want all the pieces to fit into a nice Irish story. But I am finding a lot of gaps," she had said. "It was as if Agnes MacNamara's camera just broke. And stayed that way for years!" she had grumbled indignantly.

Ed could have predicted these so-called gaps. And yes, it did have to do with Agnes. It was more than her camera that broke when Wil left to search for work.

One day, Ed and Jack were out fishing on Pawtuckaway. Jack eluded to the fact that his father's death was never solved. He blamed illness and the dangers of the railroads. Wil MacNamara did travel jumping on and off trains, like so many others of the thirties, and Jack wanted it to remain that way. He seemed satisfied not knowing. Sally apparently was not — not the best legacy to leave to Meghan.

Ed's relationship started with Ted, but ended with Ed's parents: Sally and Jack. It covered fifty years. Sally had wanted Ted to take what was left of the family relics over to England as if afraid that Jack would just as soon destroy them all. She wanted to save the family records. Ed just couldn't figure out why.

He poured the rest of the beer he had been sipping into the kitchen sink. He and Ted rarely drank alone. He decided to let Meghan have her research. He would listen and support her, to a point. He wasn't family. He decided at that moment to bide his time. It wasn't up to him to tell all. He'd wait and see before disclosing what might have been figured out already. Maybe they all had it wrong anyway.

CHAPTER 11

Scrapbooking

2014

The scrapbooking club met in Hampton Hills at Betty Beaudreau's house. Alice Finch had given Meghan the address, which wasn't difficult to find. Gathering up her largest pile of photos, she decided to get started with the group. She hoped that more experienced scrapbookers could direct her in her efforts to select and categorize some of her more difficult photos.

A half dozen cars lined the driveway of the Beaudreaus. At six o'clock, plenty of daylight remained. It was a bit awkward coming alone, but Alice assured her that this was what she needed to help her get a better handle on the immense job Sally and Agnes had left her. The companionship would also do her good.

Armed with an oversized, brown box, Meghan followed the sound of voices coming from the back porch. She tapped lightly on the screened door, and headed down a short hall. Before her sat a long oak table covered with papers and half-empty albums opened to blank pages. The heads of the ladies went up and they nodded for her to come in.

"Hello there. You must be Meghan O'Reilly, Alice's friend," a friendly female voice said.

A silver-haired woman rose from among the smiling faces and approached with an extended hand. She quickly led Meghan to a place at the table. Each woman gave Meghan their name and Meghan smiled back.

The ladies quickly returned to their own projects. She felt ill-prepared. They were equipped with jagged scissors, colorful paper, acid-free sheets, miniature edge cutters, and theme-oriented albums. All she had at hand were some pinking shears and a basic leather-bound album.

But Betty immediately put Meghan at ease.

"All albums are unique. They need not be all ribbons and fancy. I sometimes use gift wrapping paper," she admitted with a chuckle. "As long as I like the outcome, I'm satisfied. I really wonder who will take much interest in it in the future anyway. I do it for the sheer joy. Relax and have fun."

Betty patted Meghan on the shoulder. Meghan took a deep breath.

One of the ladies looked up, and without taking her hands out of her scissors, asked Meghan about her collection. "Is there one special occasion you'd like to commemorate? Or is there an era you are focusing on?" she asked Meghan.

The women at the table began to explain what the theme of their collection of photos represented. One was laying matching pink borders on an album for her new granddaughter. Another woman was organizing all the candid pictures taken at a recent wedding of her niece. Masses of colorfully printed background sheets could be seen laid out in coordinated shades, ready for insertion. Meghan thought about the huge array of topics, faces, and eras surrounding her box. Where should she begin?

"Mine are from my father's family. I have photographs from about fifty years. They were left to me by my mother, Sally, and her mother-in-law, Agnes MacNamara."

Betty left the room to put on water for tea. The smell of just-baked cookies emanated from the galley kitchen located behind the dining room.

She returned looking over the shoulders of all her guests, commenting on the color combinations or on the angle of the various images.

No one spoke for a minute. Meghan's job seemed rather confusing and enormous compared to theirs.

"I have brought along basically seven individual categories," Meghan began. "There is the one for Jack, his brothers Mike and Ted, another for Jack and Sally, then the one that seems to reflect the holidays, a summer collection, weddings, and sporting events. Some overlap," she added with a sigh.

Betty placed a cup of Chai tea beside Meghan and sat down. "We all started somewhere," she admitted. "You have years of history here. Who was the camera buff?" Betty wondered.

"Agnes. She took most of them. My mother is the one who tried to consolidate them with a journal. But there is still much that has no identification at all."

Suddenly, a woman in a sea-green scarf got up from her chair and came around to where Meghan was placing her piles of old pictures. "I knew an Agnes MacNamara. She was a friend of my mother's," she said brightly.

She picked up one of Meghan's pictures and stared at the faces. She picked up another and replaced it in its pile. Then she sat beside Meghan. "I might be able to be of help. I'm Patty."

Patty pushed the piles back and made another clean space. Slowly, with little effort, she pointed out background details to Meghan. She didn't focus on the faces as much as the hints given around the people, noticing styles of dress, hairdos, cars even and structures caught by the camera. She began to place the images in decades.

"My mother used to wear her hair like that. I have one similar in another album." She got up and lifted the album from the bottom of her bag to show Meghan. "See this. It was about 1928. This was taken prior to the Depression. This would be closer to 1935. Notice the car? And that one was taken right in front of my uncle's store on Elm Street. It burned down not long after. He never could get the money to rebuild." She looked off in the distance, remembering.

Patty and Meghan continued to peruse the seven piles, reassigning them by era or season. Meghan began to notice other clues in the images, details that had previously escaped her. The two hours flew by. Carefully, Meghan marked the backs of the photos, making mental notes to herself as well. Patty too seemed to be mesmerized by the things she recognized in Meghan's photos.

"I hope we didn't overwhelm you," Betty interrupted as she began to clear the table of empty teacups and used napkins. "There is no right or wrong way to do this. You will get what you need. I hope you found the activity fun!" she said with a big smile at Meghan.

Patty and Meghan were the last to leave; they helped Betty wash the cups and clean up the scraps of cuttings on the table. Meghan had not expected to find out so much.

"I get lost in faces," Meghan told Patty as they headed for their cars.

Patty smiled thoughtfully. "I spent my early childhood in Manchester. We moved away and rarely visited after 1929. We loved it there, but my father found work elsewhere, and we had to move to a smaller house. I remember so much about it. And funny that my mother knew your grandmother. Some of my happiest memories were made around where the MacNamaras had lived."

Patty gave Meghan a quick hug. Meghan thanked her for all her insight.

"I hope you come again," Patty called as she closed the door of her blue Impreza.

"I am learning so much about my past," Meghan called back. *And more secrets still to reveal*, she thought. It was as if she couldn't put it down. And help seemed to come even from a stranger.

CHAPTER 12

A Birthday Dinner

2014

Meghan's mother-in-law Sally MacNamara posed and leaned against the trunk of an old oak tree. The background was otherwise similar to any number of photos in the collection. Sally looked young in cut-off jeans, white tee-shirt, and sneakers; the photograph was probably taken in the late 1940s. The slightly curling image sat on the kitchen table between Meghan and Ed Shea.

"This slaw is delicious. What are these seeds?" Ed inquired as he continued to chew.

"I added sunflower seeds," Meghan replied, picking one up between her thumb and forefinger.

Ed had finally taken her up on her invitation to celebrate his September birthday. It was early October, but she decided to go with a summertime menu: chicken kabobs on the grill, mixed vegetables steamed in aluminum foil and a rice pilaf side dish. As an afterthought, she had added what she called California slaw. Was she subconsciously trying to get Ed to tell her more about his recent stay there?

Ed had decided to avoid any unnecessary talk about his own recent findings among his wife's collection of photographs. He spoke regularly with Ted and had been vague about Meghan's investigations into the

MacNamara family. Ted's visit seemed to have added more interest about Jack's parents. Ed didn't like to be the bearer of information that might be better left alone. He gazed at the photo of Sally, nodded, and put it down.

"It's funny to come over by land. It gets dark so early now on the lake, so I took the jeep. When I drove down your road, I noticed the old birdhouse still hanging on that limb." Ed smiled and looked Meghan directly in her eyes.

"It was my mother's," Meghan answered absently.

"Yeh, I know. I made it," he admitted.

"You did?"

A look of puzzlement washed over her face.

"The one way up in the pine tree with the aged copper roof?"

Meghan put down her fork, recalling that he made them and how his daughter, Kate, had been selling them at craft fairs. Meghan had bought one from her over the summer.

"I knew that it had hung there for a long time, but didn't know it was one of yours. You know how I've been sorting memorabilia and pictures? Do you know when you made it?" As she spooned more rice and slaw onto Ed's plate, she kept her ears perked up at this bit of information.

"Sure. Let me think. I usually work on birdhouses in late fall and winter. I had a friend offer me some nice sheets of copper one fall, and added them to some of my houses. It's hard to remember exactly, but you and Ted were long gone. I would have been seeing your folks more at the lake and at the association meetings. I'd guess around 1985." He nodded satisfied.

"Sally loved birds. She had bird motifs on her stationery. She hung suet up all winter for them. I still forget how far back your relationship spans with my parents." She swallowed hard. There were so many images now swimming around in her head. Ed would be a great source of knowledge in matching up the puzzles left to her by Agnes and Sally.

They ate for a few minutes in silence.

"So how is everything back in Arizona?" Ed finally asked.

"Good. My house is rented. My neighbors knew a young couple stationed there who decided to rent rather than purchase. It gives me time to finish here and to see out the year." Meghan rose to clear the table.

Ed also stood, swept the soiled napkins, and carried his plate to the sink. He rinsed his utensils. Another silence fell between them.

They had not spent much time together since their separate vacations. All summer, their time had been shared with boat rides, visits to Manchester theatres, dinners out and of course their early morning excursions in the kayaks. Meghan felt the awkwardness between them, telling herself that it was just their preoccupations with their own lives. As soon as she returned, the family project of writings and albums had become central to her.

"Ed, I'd like to take down the old birdhouse and see if it needs repairing," Meghan began.

Ed's back was toward her. He brushed off his hands over the trash basket and tossed in the empty container of mayonnaise. He hesitated and cleared his throat. "I have a friend coming to visit next week," Ed stated quietly.

"Oh," Meghan managed to say.

Again, a silence fell between them. Max sat watching the floor, hoping to catch some fallen treat.

"Yes. I'd be happy to take a look at it. It did look a bit beaten up after all these years hanging on that branch. Just not right now." He smiled weakly.

The easiness of the past summer was gone. Ed offered no more information either about the upcoming guest or the photo of Sally that remained propped up against the napkin holder on the table. Meghan didn't pursue either, but her thoughts kept intruding. There was no planning taking place here. Something had changed between them.

"I've lined up a few projects to get started at the camp. Now that I'm really retired, I will actually get some done. I'm mostly clearing and thinning out. I have been keeping in touch with some old acquaintances and reconnected with a couple of them while I visited my sister. One lives right in the same town!"

Meghan knew rambling when she heard it. She just listened. She had been really looking forward to this dinner, but this unexpected turn of events had her somewhat perplexed. She'd have to hold on to her questions for now — and her sense of being slighted.

Suddenly, Ed made his way toward the camp door. He smiled and nodded politely in her direction. "Thanks so much for dinner. It was great. Are you working on the upcoming reunion at Alan Shepard?" he asked.

"I'm not sure. There have been emails reminding me. I haven't committed, yet." Meghan tried to sound upbeat.

Grabbing his jacket, Ed again commented on the nice evening. Meghan walked him out to the porch and waved as he drove off.

What had she done? What had happened in California? She walked dumbly back inside and picked up the photo again.

Sitting down at the empty table, she studied the face of the smiling woman in it. It remained a puzzle for now. Just how well did Ed Shea know Jack and Sally? She could see nothing in the image to warrant any unusual reaction. But that wasn't the reason for her feelings.

Perhaps Ed was seeing someone else. After all, they had no spoken commitment to each other. Perhaps the image of Sally reminded him of something. He was often quite private in his thoughts. Meghan left the subject about the past and found herself very present on the lake. She sat on the couch and wrapped herself tightly in one of Sally's old quilts.

For the first time since arriving on Pawtuckaway Lake, there was a chill in the air. Meghan turned on the television to distract her racing thoughts.

CHAPTER 13

Charmed Lives

1927

During his stay at the lake, Kevin, Meghan's son, had set up email for her. She felt obligated to take him up on the offer since she was often forgetting to recharge her cell phone. Her brother Ted and her grown children wanted to be able to stay in touch with her, reminding her that there was a wider world outside of Pawtuckaway Lake. She had not felt the need to use it until October arrived and Ed's visits became scarce. But today, it was back to yet another set of photos she found herself focused on. These were in a collection that included news clippings.

The picture at hand had been taken from a few yards away, but Agnes must have had a pretty sophisticated camera because the faces were very easy to recognize. And this particular shot was not posed.

A tall man was caught with both his arms extended wide. The man next to him pointed up into the sky. In a half circle facing the men, three boys stood in apt attention. Meghan knew them all: Mike MacNamara at about age eighteen, brother Ted at about fifteen and young Jack probably about six years old. Agnes must have been observing the scene and, as was her nature, must have grabbed her camera and snapped the moment. The year "1927" appeared on the reverse side of the photo. Here was her family of men.

It was one of those perfectly recorded days, because there was even an entry in Agnes' diary to correspond. The day and date revealed even further the significance of this day, with a yellowed newspaper clipping attached. Meghan placed all the materials on the table and stepped back in time. In her sloping handwriting, Agnes' diary read:

> "May 21, 1927
>
> On this day, the men were full of excitement. Every topic they reveled in drew them to this little exchange. I could feel their spirits soaring. I went out to hang sheets and met Maureen Donahue. We both had read the morning headlines and were all following the story. Our husbands and sons couldn't get enough."

Locally, the Manchester Board of Mayor and Alderman had allocated $15,000 toward a new airport. Some eighty-four acres of land near Pine Island pond would soon be the site of two 1800-foot-long runways. And soon a terminal for passengers would be constructed.

Ford was to replace the Tin Lizzie with a Model A automobile. Henry Ford had announced that after selling twenty million cars he had a better auto to sell. The MacNamaras owned a Model T, as did many of their neighbors.

Since both the MacNamaras and the Donahues owned radios, the news of the day traveled far, not just across lines of communication, but across fences as well. As exciting as the arrival of an airport in the Queen City was the greater success of the airplane in world news. Charles Lindbergh had flown solo across the Atlantic on board the Spirit of St. Louis in thirty-three hours and thirty-nine minutes, and would become the United States' roving ambassador. Air flight was becoming a reality and would change not just local geography, but the world.

Added to Agnes' diary was a small note:

"Wil presented me with a tiny sterling silver airplane to add to my growing charm bracelet. It was no real occasion, just to celebrate the events."

Meghan wondered what ever became of it. But at that moment, all their lives were in suspended animation; none knew what was just around the next corner — a happy wife enjoying her beloved hobby, young men thrilled with planes and cars, a decade still soaring with possibilities. Here was one small family at the very crossroads of history and Agnes had thought to report on it.

Meghan felt a tinge of sadness and obligation. This was more than just the tale of one Irish family; it was the story of many families. She was the remaining MacNamara woman to put all the varied pieces together. There were so many gaps, but when it all came together like this, she felt inspired to continue. What better use of her time than this? The women of her family wanted their story told. She wouldn't let them down.

CHAPTER 14

Summer is Over

2014

E d's boat pulled away from shore. He'd hardly spent any time with Meghan since returning from California. It was as if he was in another world, not just living on the other side of Pawtuckaway Lake. Something had changed. Did he have second thoughts about retiring on the lake, or just about her?

"Brought you some nice sugar pumpkins." Ed had smiled warmly at Meghan and placed the orange gourds on the shore. "They're perfect for cooking or just displaying," he had added.

Again, he kept his distance. She expected him to place them inside. He made no such gesture to go in that direction.

"Looking forward to my retirement party? It will be great to see everyone, Ed especially! Don't you think?" Ed offered.

What could she say? The conversation was so general. He made no effort to engage or to visit. All her plans to involve him in her photo investigation had seemed futile. He was in a rush to leave and to keep things casual.

"I've unearthed more pictures," she had offered. "Maybe you might recognize some of the people."

"Sure. I'll definitely get back to you." Then he pointed at the boat. "Time to get the old girl out of the water. There'll be ice on the lake before you know it."

Ed took his boat carefully around the edge of the dock, waved, and roared away, leaving Max and Meghan to watch as he disappeared.

Meghan shrugged.

"Max, my buddy. There's something odd here. Don't you think?"

Max and she headed up to the camp. Her hopes of Ed's help would have to wait, but Agnes' journal continued to draw her back to the boxes of archives.

This entry read:

> "Jack has a childhood loss. He creates fantasy stories
> about the whereabouts of his father. It's easier to let him
> think Wil was off on some adventure."

It was dated 1934. And from the other notes, Meghan had concluded that Wil was gone about eighteen months by then. He must have been absent as he searched for work. Between about 1932 and 1937, there was an obvious gap in both the order of the journal and the sequence of photos. She had about fifty odd pictures that matched up with nothing. The quality of the pictures had declined too, and many were unmarked. History made the story clear, but what was happening to the MacNamaras themselves remained a mystery. Obviously, life reflected the times. Agnes had little time for her passion. Her diary entries had less content. Her camera must have been stored away. Her Wil was gone.

Meghan held up one picture. It was the most revealing. It hardly seemed possible that it was even Agnes. A thin woman with dark circles stood alone on a lawn. Unpainted houses dotted the background. She wore a dress that drooped on her narrow shoulders. The smile bore no resemblance to the women seen in other shots. Courage, not happiness, forced the expression on her face. Agnes looked tight and frail. The full-faced, pretty mother of Jack was gone, replaced by a woman full of worry, worn by the uncertain era of Depression.

Meghan wondered who took the picture, since most of the others were the work of Agnes herself. But someone must have insisted on putting her on the other side of the lens. Meghan lined up the images that had no obvious chronology. But she did notice one thing: Jack's handwriting had begun to show up on many of them. She knew it well. Dad was left-handed, and his script leaned decidedly backward. She needed more dates, and they were consistently the work of Agnes. Jack's additions were random, but helpful. It took the work of Agnes, Sally, Jack, and Meghan to accurately mark the appropriate timing of piles of images.

She wouldn't totally rule out the help of Ed Shea, yet. He had the right to privacy and to deal with his retirement in his own way. But she just knew that he knew a lot about the MacNamaras and would be an important resource. She just wished that he would come out of this stage, or whatever it was. She needed his help.

And she missed him too.

CHAPTER 15

A Retirement and a Return

2014

The faces of youngsters, her own youthful image included, looked back as Meghan took one last look at the 1974 Alan Shepard yearbook. She wanted to be able to refer to as many attendees by name, and thought a quick peek before going to Ed's retirement party might help. For weeks, her focus had been on images from the long ago past, but tonight the events of only one year would be her focus: her stint as a substitute under Principal Ed Shea. It was his night, but she knew it was special for her as well.

The soft sound of shower water and the fresh smell of lathered soap emanated from the bathroom where Ted prepared for his friend's party. He had arrived with little time to spare and had dashed down the hall dragging a suit still sealed in plastic. Meghan had already spent a fair amount of time putting together an appropriate outfit for the occasion. In fact, she had bought a new dress.

Ed had phoned only once since his last visit and had disclosed little about the guest list.

"There will be staff, friends, family and many who either attended Alan Shepard or had family members who had. Seating is open," he'd added.

His daughter Kate and grandson Dan would be there. He mentioned a cousin flying in from California. Ed's long-time secretary, Louise Beauchemin, from the school, had helped arrange many details for his guests. She had sold over one hundred tickets herself.

The call was short.

"So glad you and Ted are coming," he had added before signing off.

Meghan had bumped into Louise at the market the day before. "It's going to be so odd without Ed," Louise decried. "I wish I could retire. But I have to work a few more years. The place feels empty and we've only been back in session a few weeks! He was great to work for."

Meghan had hugged her and said that Ed must finally be ready to let go of work. Meghan added that she knew he was looking forward to his long-earned retirement. "You will be the principal this year. We all know that you could run the place if you had to," Meghan kidded.

Louise pushed her carriage full of produce out the door, a huge smile lingering on her pink lips.

All this was running through her mind as Meghan waited for her brother to appear from the bedroom. She was relieved that he was able to get time from work to fly over from England again. He had just been at the camp over the summer. Obviously, Ted had a good rapport with his boss. She just liked the idea that he would be her date for the night.

Ted emerged wearing a soft, grey jacket, khaki slacks, pale blue oxford, and a blue striped tie of complementary shades. His hair was slightly damp and stuck up in the back. She approached him and reached her right hand up to tame a cowlick. His shoes shone of new leather. He smiled approvingly at her.

"Well, don't you just look lovely, tonight." He smirked affectionately at her and placed a kiss on her cheek. "My wife likes that pale shade of purple too. It looks good on you both."

Meghan wore a set of sterling earrings and matching necklace, both adorned with marcasite. The jewelry, Meghan had learned recently, was worn often as a substitute for diamonds during the Depression. They sparkled in the early evening light, flattering both her tanned skin and pastel outfit. She felt like she had one foot in the distant past and the other in the recent past. Tonight though, it was just three friends celebrating a landmark: the passing into another stage of life — their own.

"Are we set?" Ted asked.

"Ready as can be expected," Meghan responded hooking her arm into her brother's.

The drive over was quiet. Ted appeared focused on the road, while Meghan wondered whom she might encounter at the school. Ed Shea was the star tonight. She and Ted were welcome guests. She watched as most of the traffic appeared to be going in the same direction.

The parking lot outside Alan Shepard High School was almost full. A bright red banner draped over the front of the building read:

"This vacation is the best of all . . .
Happy Retirement!!!!!"

Ted got out and quickly rushed over to let his sister out of the rental car; the red truck didn't seem appropriate for tonight. The rental was a white convertible with black top, leather interior and shiny hubcaps. They ran the air so as not to mess up Meghan's hair. The air outside was warm for October.

"We have to go for a top-down ride before you turn this in," she told Ted as they disembarked.

She remembered her first trip over to the school the previous spring, driving the red truck. She had sat outside remembering her days there. Here she was again in an official capacity and dressed for the occasion. No flannel shirt tonight.

Inside, the caterers had done up the library. Bookshelves were pushed back, linen covered the tables, and a petition separated the references area. Roses in vases sparked in the candlelight on each table. Carafes of red and white wine sat in the center of the room with dozens of stemware. China plates sat at each place setting: cream and gold trimmed. How elegant it all looked. One hardly recognized where they were.

Waiters and waitresses holding appetizer trays stopped to offer Ted and Meghan some scallops wrapped in bacon, tiny quiches, stuffed crab-meat mushrooms, and meat balls. White napkins emblazoned with a golden "S" accompanied these treats. This was quite an evening of celebration.

Almost immediately, Meghan felt eyes upon her as people headed her way.

"Mizzy Mac, this is my wife, Ellen," one tall man called out.

"Remember period three? We did all those papers on our family history?" another balding man announced.

"Ms. Mac, we are so glad you came!" a small blonde woman blurted out.

Meghan felt right at home. So many former students were in attendance. Ted took it all in as his friend and sister mixed with the crowd.

"I just got a sign from Ed. Be right back," Ted whispered to Meghan. He headed over to where the principal stood among snapping cameras and cell phones. Ted acted as the camera person as others handed him their equipment. Multiple group photos were shot.

"I should have thought to bring my own camera," Meghan said to one of the guests. "It seems to be in our family blood." She had to chuckle thinking of Agnes.

Louise Beauchemin moved about the room stopping to give directions to the various workers. She wanted the food hot, drinks cold and for everyone to have a chance to talk to the guest of honor. Many began to make their way to various tables, and from somewhere, music could be heard. The noise level diminished a little, but chatter filled the library as guests clinked glasses, laughed and shook hands. Many hugged, tears in their eyes, smiles on their lips. This was a preview to the official reunion yet to come, Meghan thought.

Suddenly, Ted had Meghan by the arm and was leading her to a table.

Ed walked to the podium with Louise. She was whispering something to him. He nodded and stepped aside as they searched the crowd for someone. Jimmy Norris was spotted and quickly hailed to come to the microphone. Ed Shea took a seat at the head table, and those guests left standing began to take seats. Ed waved in the direction of Meghan and Ted. The smell of hot food drifted into the room. Salads came first, accompanied by pumpkin bread and hot cinnamon rolls.

Ted stood up and headed for the head table, leaving Meghan to greet the other diners as they asked to join her at her table. Meghan always liked the idea of unassigned seating. That way you could meet new people.

"May we join you?" a couple that looked vaguely familiar asked Meghan.

"Absolutely." She nodded.

Ted returned with two glasses of champagne.

"What a great turnout. Such a tribute to a solid guy!" the man to Meghan's left commented.

"I'm Meghan. And this is my brother, Ted."

"Nice to meet you," the woman added. "I'm Sarah and this is my husband, Alex."

They chatted as others filled in the empty seats around their table.

"I know you," Alex suddenly blurted out to Ted. "You are a MacNamara. I knew Jack. You look just like him."

By now Meghan had grown used to such exchanges, but to Ted, whose life was spent abroad, it was an unexpected comment.

"I live in London. I rarely meet anyone who knows me, never mind my family," Ted responded with a big grin.

The man went on to tell Meghan and Ted about his connection to their father.

"Jack wrote articles for my paper. I own the *Hampton Hills Gazette*. He did my fishing column for years. Great guy. Sorry. We miss him at the paper."

Sarah touched Meghan's hand and nodded. Alex nodded solemnly.

"It's great to be here. Dad had a lot of connections in his fishing world." Ted smiled over at Meghan.

A momentary stillness crossed her brother's otherwise smiling face. They sat quietly for a few seconds.

Jimmy Norris was once again at the microphone. Meghan noticed Ed's daughter Kate had taken her seat beside her father. Dan settled in next to her. Meghan informed Ted that Jimmy had been a former student of hers. The sounds of voices subsided as Jimmy began the evening's ceremony.

"Welcome. Thank you all for coming. I see so many familiar faces. Many of you taught here, attended here, or grew up nearby. And doesn't our library look amazing tonight?"

He glanced at the many in white, attending to the guests.

"Many thanks to all of you who made this evening happen. Special thanks to Louise Beauchemin. She remains the heart and soul of our school. What would we have done without her all these years?"

The room erupted in applause.

"Please feel free to mix and mingle while dinner is served. For your entertainment and for a trip down memory lane, we will be running a film on the screen behind me. It is a running commentary of about forty years of memories associated with our alma mater. Sit back and enjoy!"

Jimmy sat, and the images began to pass overhead.

The room quieted down as scene after scene rolled by: new construction, dances, basketball tournaments, snow covered football fields, graduations, fund raisers, marching bands, pep rallies, holiday parades . . . Fingers pointed, and oohs and aahs resounded. Many saw themselves among the moments. Lips quivered; eyes filled up. Hands reached up to mouths.
For the next half hour, yesterday became today. Like the pages of a yearbook, the video relayed the story of one American high school under the leadership of one capable captain.

Ed Shea didn't eat much. Among the pictures were many of Ed's wife, Joanne. She was not the only one, however, whose face brought guests back to another decade. Meghan and all in attendance saw themselves.

When the tape ended, strawberry shortcake drizzled with maple syrup arrived. Coffee and tea steaming with heat accompanied the rattling of plates and forks. Meghan caught a quick look at Ed's face; it must have hurt from all the smiling. She got up to go to the restroom when a strange woman walked directly in her path.

"Sam. There you are," the woman said over Meghan's shoulder.

Meghan almost stumbled. Surely, he had every right to attend. He had taught at Alan Shepard longer than she had. Meghan turned her head in the direction of the woman's eyes, prepared to act casually around Sam Norton.

Instead, the woman gave Sam Campbell and Judy big hugs.

"How's Max?" Sam mouthed to Meghan.

Relieved, Meghan gave Sam and Judy a thumbs-up sign and continued on toward the restroom.

Ed had made his way over to where she and Ted had sat and shook hands with Alex and Sarah. Ted listened while the couple explained that both their children and grandchildren attended Alan Shepard. Ted offered to help haul Ed's many gifts out to the car later.

"You can come over and get them tomorrow," Ted offered.

Ed moved on toward the reception line that had formed at the exit from the library. Louise successfully herded him and his guests in that direction. While Ed shook hands and enjoyed all the gratitude from his years as their administrator, Ted, Meghan and Dan carried wrapped packages to the trunk of the convertible. The overflow went into Ed's trunk.

Before heading out, Meghan caught up with Louise and once again complimented her on the affair. "You did a terrific job here tonight. So many great times. So many wonderful memories."

"It wasn't hard to recruit help," Louise admitted, her eyes tearing up. "The end of an era," she added with a sniffle.

Jimmy caught Meghan's eye just as she and Ted reached the rental and were about to squeeze in with all the loot.

"More to come, Mizzy Mac," Jimmy called to her. "Our reunion is next!"

Meghan smiled and wondered if that were as true as it sounded.

"Talk soon!" she called back and settled into the front seat next to her brother.

The night air had chilled. No top-down tonight. But the memories made the interior of the convertible feel warm and all the world seem right.

CHAPTER 16

After the Affair

October 10–13, 2014

The retirement party was over. Funny how anticipation is often as much a part of an event as the event itself. Meghan and Ted drove back to the lake chatting about the various people they'd met, and Ed's obvious pleasure in the whole occasion.

"He was so tickled," Ted commented. "So many people came to either thank him for his commitment, or to reminisce. Our trunk is full!"

"It took him twice to actually retire," Meghan nodded as she spoke. "His secretary, Louise, told me that she had planned the celebration before, but had to call it all off when Ed decided not to leave."

"He wasn't ready. What with losing Joanne and his routine at school." Ted paused and then as an afterthought went on. "It's hard to know when it is the right time." He looked over at his sister. "He was happy you came."

The last sentence hung in the air between them. Meghan wanted to respond, but decided not to. Instead, she changed the subject.

"Who were the people in that group picture you took?" she inquired.

"I guess some old staff members, some already retired. One was a coach who has been pretty sick but didn't want to miss it all." He paused. "Did you see Sam Campbell and Judy?"

"Yes, yes, I did. I didn't get a chance to talk to them much."

Meghan looked ahead remembering her moment of confusion and panic over the chance that the *other* Sam had been there.

"Of course, Sam attended Alan Shepard and is also Ed's car mechanic." She tried to sound casual even as her neck felt heat crawling at the thought. "So glad you remembered to bring a camera. It must run in the family, all this photography. You know, our grandmother Agnes was our family shutterbug!"

This was her opportunity to broach the subject. Ted picked up her cue.

"How is that project of yours coming, anyway? Were there a lot of pictures among the stuff I sent you in the box?" he inquired innocently.

"Well, there were. And so many I cannot identify. They were taken long before I was born. And some were not taken by the same person," Meghan said with a note of frustration in her voice. "I hope you might help me with some of those."

There, she'd said it. Her secret investigation into diaries, journals, and photos needed a second pair of eyes from within the family on them. The box was left to her, but she couldn't imagine that additional assistance was out of the question. The experience at the scrapbooking club clearly taught her that.

They were reaching Mountain Road, passing darkened houses. It was after midnight. By the time they had collected up all of Ed's gifts and said their goodbyes, the library was returning to its original look. Bookshelves would need to be rolled back into place. The parking lot would be emptied, and the landmark occasion would soon be a thing of the past.

The short road leading to the camp came up on their right. Ted drove slowly. The trunk's contents shifted.

"I'm beat," Ted announced as he stopped the car beside the camp. "How about we unpack all this in the morning?"

"That works for me," Meghan agreed, although she wasn't ready to turn in yet.

Quickly, Ted made his way up the pull-down ladder to his childhood cave. Meghan watched his long legs and sturdy shoulders disappear into the small retreat.

"Goodnight," he called back.

"See you in the morning," she responded. "Sleep in. No reason to get up early."

She made her way down the dark hall turning into her parents' bedroom. Almost remotely, Meghan headed toward the table holding the photo pile marked "Unknown." *Why are some of these considered important?* she pondered. *Who were they?* Staring hard at the smiling faces staring back at her, she asked them aloud.

"Why you? What do you know? Why did Sally save you? Why did Agnes want you among the close MacNamara clan?"

Max wandered in and flopped down with a big sigh. Finding the porch door open, he must have wandered back from the Finches'.

"Max, we didn't mean to neglect you all night!" Meghan apologized.

He came over for a long patting, but soon curled up to watch her in this habit she had of moving papers around on top of the desk.

The image of the 1974 yearbook continued to pop into her head. She wanted to look at the faces she knew. She drew it from the back of the bookshelf. Snuggling into her father's big, well-worn leather reading chair, she began to turn the pages and pick up where the evening video had left off.

Among the familiar people was, of course, Ed. Here, he was presented awards for academic achievements and trophies for athletic victories. Huge plaques covered many of the group pictures.

Jimmy Norris showed up repeatedly: playing on the golf team, running cross-country, skiing dressed in warm winter gear, posing with a cute female classmate.

Then she turned to the staff section. She and Sam stood together in the stacks of the school library directing students' attention to research for some science reports they were coordinating. Another depicted a quiet moment caught unexpectedly with Sam and Meghan bent over an open encyclopedia together, totally absorbed in the moment. And of course, Meghan's favorite one with Sam Norton tandem with the statue of the golf-playing astronaut, Alan Shepard, in the school courtyard.

"The power of a picture," Meghan said out loud.

No words were needed to read the expressions. For weeks, she had been immersed in hundreds of such moments belonging to the MacNamara archives. This yearbook told the story of just one year in her young life. The provenance of the family was rich in history, a photo collection valuable only to those who knew the stories. And still, she had only meager elements of the entire tale. What she needed was the mortar to strengthen the many bricks. Someone must know more than either the diary or journal revealed. What tied them all together?

Suddenly, Meghan's eyes felt very heavy. She rose to remove her fancy clothes. Carefully, she replaced the yearbook back on the shelf behind the leather chair and headed down the hall to her room. The evening had been full of memories, and her head couldn't organize any more. Ted and Ed were her next resource. But for now, what she really needed was sleep.

CHAPTER 17

A Shower of Gifts

November 13, 2014

A
ll was still and dark at the Finches' next door. Meghan knew that they had planned to attend Ed's retirement party, and their absence seemed odd. She had inquired once she noticed they hadn't shown up, but had been unable to get any solid answers from anyone. Ted found out only that it had been some kind of emergency. And Ed was too involved with his many guests for her to speak to him about it.

Like his father, Ted was an early riser. She woke the next morning to the sound of closing doors as Ted hauled in arms full of festively wrapped boxes from his rental car. By the time she was fully awake and had wandered into the living room, her couch and floor area were piled high with well-wishers' offerings. More envelopes covered the side chairs and tabletop.

"Ed said he'd call. He'll be by for all this today," Ted shouted back as he headed out for another load of gifts. Max followed closely behind.

Picking up some of Ed's cards, and pushing them aside, Meghan began to make room for breakfast. With the car emptied, Ted and Max had headed down to the beach for a swim. It would be a quick dip in the cool water.

What was it that brought the boy out in grown men at the lake? Soon, Ted stood dripping wet on the shore, tossing a stick back out into the water for a willing canine. Max bound puppy-like out into the lake again and again. Poor Max must have felt abandoned the night before, with the Finches absent and them out at the retirement party. The dog showed up soon after she and Ted arrived back the night before, curling up for the night at the threshold of her bedroom. It had become Max's favorite sleeping spot. He had two homes, but if Meghan were in, this was his first choice.

A tinkling sound emitted from Meghan's cell phone. She grabbed it.

"Hi, there." Ed's familiar voice sounded cheery. "Did you have a nice time?"

"Oh, yes. Very nice. What a great evening. I recognized so many faces!" she admitted.

"Am I calling too early?"

"No. We were up. Actually, Ted and Max are swimming. And we have a lot of loot from your admirers," Meghan teased.

Just then, Ted and Max stepped up on the outside porch.

"Can you toss me a dry towel?" Ted called.

Meghan made her way to a pile of beach towels stored in a wicker basket in the corner of the porch. As she handed one to her brother, she pointed to the phone and mouthed, "Ed." Ted took the receiver with one hand and proceeded to dry off his legs with the other.

"Hey. Quite a celebrity in these parts," Ted began.

Max shook himself violently, and found a sunny spot to lay down on the outer deck. Ted headed inside, talking to Ed as he went. Meghan felt that ache in her stomach as the two picked up like old schoolmates, leaving her out again.

She began to plan. She wanted to use the memories of the two of them while she had them together. They could identify the unknowns in some of her photos, or at least point out things she seemed to be missing. Being older, they would remember further back, she hoped.

"Invite Ed over for lunch," Meghan whispered into her brother's ear as he passed her; he was already half dressed in sweats.

Ted headed down the hallway and then returned to hang his wet towel out on the porch railing. So many habits were entrenched in them. Was he aware that they all did the same thing? He talked away and, out of habit, hung his wet suit in the bathroom and scooped up another dry towel to dry his hair.

Meghan went into the kitchen to see what she could muster up for food. She had cold cuts, cheese, rye bread, and pickle to start. There might be an open bag of chips. Mentally, she was already planning what pictures she wanted their input on. It was easier to talk when eating, at least in the MacNamara household.

* * *

Within an hour, Ed was sitting in the living room of the MacNamara camp opening packages and slicing the sides of envelopes. Like a bridal shower, Meghan suggested that Ted keep a running list of who gave what to Ed.

"Joanne would have thought of that," Ed remarked.

"You will be glad you did," Meghan called to the men from the kitchen where she had begun to place paper plates and napkins out on a clear kitchen table.

She found some olives, pickles, and celery to add to the spread, and radishes. She placed them all out on a platter with sliced tomatoes. Satisfied, she followed the men's voices into the living room.

The room resembled the scene on a Christmas morning: paper, ribbon, and tissues strewn everywhere.

"Look, a new fishing hat!" Ted announced flopping it on his friend's head.

"From my former head of Guidance," Ed called out. Ted wrote it down.

"Who gave me these?" Ed wondered, holding up a set of bright red boat cushions.

"Says the Johnsons."

"This one is a gift certificate from Tuckaway Tavern."

"That is from the former football coach, Chuck Bellemore."

The give and take went on with Meghan listening to the ongoing commentary. Ed read all the cards aloud, many comical, others quite touching. When it seemed to Meghan it was getting too serious, Max arrived to break up the mood. He grabbed a pile of wrinkled wrapping paper and gave it a good thrashing. He spit it out and shook it again.

The men chuckled at the antics.

"A cat must have sent that one," Meghan commented.

Ted shot Max an affectionate look as Max attempted to find a comfortable spot to lay down amidst the paper shreds. Finally, the dog found a nice cushy spot in the middle of the room and flopped there. There was a sound like crinkling leaves and a thud as he settled in.

The process of opening and recording went on until all the gifts had been opened and the list of matching names completed.

"Come eat," Meghan invited.

The three moved to the table. Max sat nearby listening to sounds of squirting mustard, shaking ketchup and crunching chips. Soda decompressed, and Meghan handed the men plastic tumblers full of ice. She now had their mouths full. Lunch was underway.

"You guys need to help me make sense of some of these pictures," she began. "I have photographs taken before I was born. And since you two have a few years on me," she grinned at them both, "you might know who they are."

Taking a long sip of her soda, Meghan anxiously lifted a brown cardboard box over to the empty kitchen chair.

"We'll do our best," Ted offered.

Ed nodded.

Meghan laid photos out on the extra leaf of the table. She held others up in front of them for a closer look. Patiently, she waited for their comments. They munched and studied her collection.

"This one was a neighbor of yours," Ed pointed out. "They were the Friedmans. They moved away when we were in high school."

"Yeh. I remember. Their daughter was beautiful." Ed gave Ted a look. He nodded.

Meghan made a mark on her blank pad.

"This one was when I got that cat out of Sully's tree. I almost broke my arm. My mother was so mad." Ed made a low groan. He held the picture up and stared closely. "Why keep it? Mom really was upset at me for climbing up so far, but she took a picture of it anyway. Sully's mother was all over me for saving Crispy. That was her cat's name."

Meghan had never heard this story.

The two men leaned forward as Meghan produced another stack. She listened to their own memories of related stories, making mental notes. Some sounded vaguely familiar, but others were stories she did not recall. She would treat them with equal value. The very fact that pictures were shot gave them relevance.

"I'm guessing that this one was taken on one of the Sundays Dad and Mom would go to Massabesic Lake for a picnic. They liked to be near water, even then. Look how young they were! We were probably not born.

There are no fishing poles. Might be in the early 1950s or late 1940s, I would guess."

Ted smiled as he looked closer at his parents back in their heyday.

Meghan noticed that, periodically, Ed seemed to stare but make no comment. She knew that about him now. Ed was often quiet when he knew something he didn't want to say. Was it just a glimpse of his own life reflected in their shared childhoods, or was it more? Maybe he would disclose more at a later time. She hoped so.

"Want more soda?" Meghan offered.

"No, thanks. I'm good," Ed responded as he rose from his chair.

He appeared to have suddenly snapped back from his own thoughts. He got up and stretched his long legs.

"The big question is why Sally kept all these. Some seem so inconsequential. And why include people who aren't even related?" Meghan asked the men.

Ed excused himself to use their bathroom. Ted continued to mull over the last pile of pictures and to point out details that might place them in their correct context of place and time.

"My question remains — why did Mom send these all the way to me in London in the first place?" Ed said slowly.

"I'm glad you kept them," Meghan responded.

It was all she could think to say. She hadn't gotten all her inquiries answered, but this had opened up her investigation a little wider. It appeared to be her task to make sense of a lot of mismatched images. Her mother had taken great pains to conserve them, and her grandmother had contributed many pages of writing to be sure the stories were preserved. What was she to add to it, if anything?

Ed returned and looked at his watch.

"I need to get this mess out of your living room. Thanks so much for all your help. Do you have a large trash bag for the paper?"

Max got up from his crushed paper bed and yawned.

Between the three of them, the floor was cleared in minutes. They carted the items carefully out to Ed's back seat and trunk. Meghan hadn't had the chance to ask about the whereabouts of the Finches.

"So what happened to Bob and Alice?" she finally asked Ed.

"It was an accident. An old college pal of Bob's. They flew out mid-afternoon yesterday, to be there. They might be gone a few days," Ed informed them.

Meghan closed the back door of Ed's car. She surveyed the area for Max. Ed leaned out the car window as he backed out of the MacNamaras' driveway. He turned his gaze toward Ted.

"So, any chance we can get together before you head back? What time is your flight?"

"I have an afternoon flight, tomorrow," Ted said with a look of disappointment.

Meghan was just beyond earshot. Max came lolling over to see Ed off.

Ed paused. Meghan was heading over toward his car. Ted's back blocked her view, so she was unable to make out their conversation. That feeling of being left out again struck her. It was just for a split second, as they turned and smiled at her.

She heard Ted saying that he wished he had more time.

"Columbus Day isn't really seen as a holiday in England. I just couldn't miss this shindig," Ted punched Ed in the arm.

"See you soon."

Ed called back as he turned the car toward the dirt road leading away from the lake. He raised his arm raised to wave at them both, and then he disappeared into the lush, fall foliage. Ted stood for a second before heading inside the camp.

CHAPTER 18

New Discoveries

Columbus Day Weekend 2014

Muffled voices could be heard as the sun came up over the eastern edge of the lake. The soulful cry of a loon echoed over the water. Somewhere a boat motor hummed. Meghan's eyes opened slowly. *What time is it?* she wondered.

Max didn't appear. It took her a moment to get her bearings. The digital clock beside the bed glared a green number "5:00." She yawned. In the split second it took for her to come to, she remembered that Ted was here. He must be out on the beach already, and of course Max would have followed him. Rising out of bed, she moved the curtains to look out.

Ed Shea's boat sat next to the MacNamara dock, motor gurgling softly. Ed and Ted stood leaning against the posts, steam rising from cups held in their hands. Max could be seen sitting inches away.

What was so important that it could not wait until later in the day? Didn't Ted's flight leave late that afternoon? And why had she been left out? Confused, tired, and somewhat indifferent, Meghan crawled back into bed. Let them go fishing or whatever; she'd sleep in.

* * *

Just a half hour earlier, Ted's phone rang. Half-asleep he'd answered a call in what felt to him like the middle of the night.

"Julie?" he said, automatically assuming it had to be her and worrying immediately that it was one of the kids. His fears were quickly quelled.

"It's Ed. Sorry to call so early. I couldn't talk in front of your sister. Want to go out on the lake? About twenty minutes?" Ted spoke softly.

"Sure. Come on over." Ed was up and ready.

Max and Ted left the camp quietly and stood waiting on shore in the misty morning.

Ed soon arrived and handed his friend a hot coffee; the threesome departed out on the morning water. The boat headed toward the Blueberry Islands, where Ed cut the motor, dropped anchor and handed Ed a blueberry muffin.

"Just like old times," Ted chuckled, holding up the confection and pointing to the namesake behind them.

But Ed seemed in a solemn mood.

"So, why so secretive? What couldn't you say in front of my sister?" Ted wanted to know.

Ed sat down on the bench seat in the rear of the boat. He unzipped his fleece vest, stirred his coffee, and broke off a corner of his muffin. Ted watched curiously as Ed made a face and reached inside his vest, removing a large manila envelope. He handed it in a ceremonial fashion to Ted.

"What is this? More photographs? How many are there?" Ted attempted to lighten the suddenly somber mood.

Ed focused intently on his friend's face.

"It's more than that," Ed admitted.

Inside were some yellowed photos accompanied by a wad of old newspaper articles. Ted unfolded the crispy paper, careful not to tear the dry parchment. On the top could be read the date "1936." This meant nothing to him.

"Read it," Ed instructed softly. It read:

> "William T. MacNamara, born in Manchester, New Hampshire, in 1890, was found dead. A former graduate of Manchester HighSchool and former employee of the 7-20-4 Cigar Factory, MacNamara left the city in 1931. [His] whereabouts [had] remained a mystery.
>
> Cause of death was unknown at the time of printing. No services are planned. He leaves three sons, Jack, Theodore, and Michael, and his wife, the former Agnes A. Boyle, also of Manchester."

Ted was silent for a moment.

"There's more," Ed pointed to the other articles.

Ted unfolded the rest. They appeared to be roughly torn pieces of newsprint taken from out-of-town newspapers. The top article read:

> "The body of William T. MacNamara was found on the shore of the Merrimac River. It lay a few miles downstream under a trestle of the main line of the Lowell, B & M rails. Cause of death appears to be drowning."

Most of the stories were written in November of 1936. But it was the last line in one newspaper that caught Ted's eye. It read:

> "Suspected suicide."

Both men looked at one another for a moment, neither knowing what to say. Ed waited for his friend to let the information sink in.

"My father never discussed his father. And we didn't ask. He said only that Wil MacNamara died of some illness. Where did you get all this?" Ted wondered.

"Your mother Sally gave all of it to me. It was one of those times that Jack was purging old stuff. He wanted it buried with the past. She disagreed for some unknown reason. I figured it wasn't up to me to just give it to your sister. With all her excavating into the legacy of the family, it was inevitable that she would dig here. So, I thought I should give it to you first," Ed admitted with a sigh.

"Boy, what started as an innocent family search is really getting into some unexpected areas. My grandfather is one person Meghan is finding less and less data on. He vanished from the albums, the journals, and the MacNamara narrative. He isn't captured in pictures for years! But is this the reason?" Ed sounded upset.

Ted shuffled through the rest of the manila folder's contents. He found more obituaries from both Manchester, New Hampshire, and Boston, Massachusetts, areas. The papers eventually confirmed both the identity of the body and the assessment of cause of death.

The boat lobbed in the water. Loons called to one another across the empty lake, their mournful voices echoing one another.

"So, Meghan hasn't directly inquired about Wil yet?" Ted looked worried.

"No. She is at a roadblock in her effort to chronologically put all the images in order and to name all the faces. There are gaps, as she calls them, when she will turn to me or you or the ladies at scrapbooking to figure out the missing parts. She is pretty astute, but so far, she hasn't asked about any specifics on Wil. I've avoided being too informative," Ed explained.

"Funny how my mother sent this off to you, and the box off to me in England. Now that Meghan is back in the state, she seems to be the one who is supposed to sort it all out. But is she supposed to find this? And why now?"

Ed put all the old papers back inside the envelope.

Ted squeezed his empty coffee cup, and rolling up the cupcake papers, he stuffed them inside it. He looked off in the direction of the MacNamara camp. Ed began to pull in the anchor and prepare to head back.

"Well, for now, I think it's best to let it all sit. Let's see how much Meghan finds out. Oddly, it's taken an entire generation to bring this to light. What damage could it do to stall?" Ted stated flatly.

The men took seats in the front of the boat. Ed started the motor and slowly turned the boat westward. Ted tapped his childhood friend on the shoulder and smiled.

"Thanks, my friend, for telling me first. Meghan has quite a proud image of her clan, especially Jack. She would be upset to think that this was all kept secret, and how it taints her ongoing story. I hate to spoil it, yet, anyway."

"I agree," Ed nodded.

* * *

"Your dad and I met many mornings like this one to fish. Funny trying to second-guess him, years later," Ed remarked to Ted in a whisper.

Ted gave the yellow folder a gentle pat and shoved it deeper inside the front of his father's sweatshirt.

As Ed pushed the throttle forward, his boat cutting through the still water, both men's minds were back in some past place wondering why things happened the way they did, but even more wondering who was better off with a little less information. Did it really need to be revealed?

The sun was well on its way up on the back-end of Pawtuckaway Lake, its golden face reflected across the deep blue surface. The loons were silent.

A single fish broke the surface of the water, only to dive deeply into the bosom of the lake. A family secret would remain there too. At least for now.

CHAPTER 19

A Chill in the Air: Face to Face

October 2014

Ted said little about his nocturnal boating in the wee hours of Columbus Day.

"Ed just wanted to take a ride and show me where he was having some luck fishing. With guests and all at his place, he needed some time alone. He knew that if he didn't catch me early, I would be gone," Ted explained over breakfast later that morning.

But Meghan continued to feel the distance growing between her and Ed. Had the summer meant so little to him? Was her only real connection because of her brother? With the retirement party over, there was little along the way of socializing she could count on. They had made no plans to get together. So when Ted finished lunch and explained that he wanted to pick up something for Julie at the mall before he flew back to England, Meghan had to admit that the weekend was over. The season was chilling, as was her relationship with Ed.

The Finches had returned. Meghan intended to go over and pay her respects to Bob. Apparently, they had flown immediately to Florida to be at Bob's family's side, remained for the funeral, and then headed directly back. She would visit in the next few days. Max was already beating a path between the two camps.

What Meghan really wanted to do was to call Ed, but she resisted the urge.

As she had done when arriving on the lake in June, Meghan began to create a list of things she needed to do in preparation for fall. For one thing, she needed warmer clothes. There were woolen blankets stored in closets, and more quilts as well, but they might need to be dry cleaned.

Max appeared at the porch, scratching to come in.

"Well, hello. Busy with all your visits, huh?" she said as she released the latch; he pushed past her.

"I have to get ready for colder nights. Apparently, you and I are to be together through December. We will need wood brought inside, and perhaps I need to go into Manchester and buy flannel sheets. I do need a break from the photo project."

She watched as Max flopped down on the tile floor of the kitchen and listened attentively.

"I'm going to clean out the rest of Dad's bureau today. He has some nice thick woolen sweaters I may confiscate. Also, there is his barn jacket collection, which could prove very handy. I may get them cleaned as well."

She headed off into the study to begin. As she wandered down the hallway, she wondered if she could discover any more on her own with the photos and journals. Ted and Ed had been marginally helpful, but the ladies at the scrapbooking club proved to be most observant. They pointed out details she had overlooked. She looked forward to the next meeting and wondered if Alice Finch might go this time.

The top drawer of Jack's bureau was tight. Meghan wiggled both sides and yanked at the same time. One thing true of wood in a camp was its tendency to swell. Dampness affected every piece made of wood in the place. She managed to pull the drawer wide enough to reveal a plethora of Henleys' thermal long-sleeved underwear, buttons missing, some quite white, others badly yellowed. The best of them would serve as warm nightshirts for her. Jack had had the tendency to shove his clothes into drawers, leaving the back full of well-flattened items, compressed solidly against the back. She wiggled her fingers behind the clothing and poked them free. She had already organized most of these and felt satisfied with this drawer.

Meghan replaced it with a shove and pulled out the one below. Here was the assortment of crewneck sweaters she'd remembered seeing: navy, forest and charcoal grey. A few V-neck cotton pullovers were squashed behind these. Her fingers felt plastic. One sweater was still wrapped in cellophane. Using both hands, she freed it and placed it on the bed.

This package contained an old Irish knit cardigan. Large and bulky, the sight of it reminded her of the two weeks her parents had spent in Ireland for their fiftieth anniversary. She knew the meaning behind the knit. It was the Boyle design, after Sally's family. She recalled that if an Irish fisherman drowns at sea, he would be identified by the knit of his clan. Like a handsewn life vest, created just in case — she shuddered.

Opening it out, she was surprised at its size. Maybe she could wear it around the camp over the winter with a turtleneck underneath. It smelled of mothballs, and she noticed fragments of white still stuck in the collar. They appeared to be worn fragments of torn lace, not worth mending. Someone must have stored them there. Fortunately, she could detect no obvious holes in the weave of the sweater even after all these years. She liked the idea of this find. It could be aired out. Like so many items in the camp, this jumper, as the Irish called them, felt close to her past.

In one of the two small top drawers were socks made of rag wool, rolled neatly into pairs. In the other were woolen scarves and two sets of leather gloves. She pulled them all out on the floor. Among the wintery clothes was an old biscuit tin containing cufflinks and a long-discarded men's wallet. Meghan held it vertically; it still conformed to the shape of Jack's back pocket where he would have carried it.

"He hasn't used this one in years!" she told Max. From its the whitish surface, the leather looked as if it had been soaked in water.

Inside was an expired Connecticut driver's license, dated 1963. Also, there was a one- dollar bill. She lifted the bill out. It might have been the first dollar Jack had earned. Opening it, Meghan noticed a tiny photo pressed inside.

"More pictures!" Meghan sighed. "And from a man who didn't want to dwell in the past!"

It was very wrinkled. The image was hard to decipher. She took it over and flicked on a light to get a better view. The woman in the tiny photo sat crossed-legged on the steps of a fancy front porch. Behind her an oak door shone, screened windows were partially open and a green wicker chair donned a floral pillow. It was summer. The woman smiled teasingly out at the camera.

Meghan squinted and reached for a pair of her father's reading glasses to magnify the face. The woman's head tilted forward, ready to laugh, her eyes sparkling. The dress flared gracefully across her knees, like the skirt on a Christmas tree. She wore hoop earrings and a sparkling cuff on her left wrist. Next to her on the porch floor was a camera.

"Sure enough," Meghan squealed. Max wandered over to investigate.

This was a picture of the photographer herself — this had to be Agnes Boyle. This image was taken when she was eighteen or nineteen. Here was a photograph of the family shutterbug. Who took it? Probably Wil. This was Jack's own mother in her youth: vibrant, happy, alive, and probably engaged to Wil. There was no date on the back to verify any of this. But Jack had saved it. Meghan had so few such pictures of a young Agnes.

"Try as I might to put down this search for the family story, it continues to tell me its tale," Meghan said to no one.

This was where the story began. It was this woman who loved Wil MacNamara. It was this woman who captured the images Meghan had inherited. Agnes had left pages from an incomplete story written on torn notebook pages and stashed in assorted journals. She had passed her journals and photographs to Sally, and Sally had preserved them for Meghan. Decades passed between the time of this moment and the present. Why was it that Sally wanted Meghan to make sense of it all? And why did Jack selectively maintain his own memories while claiming not to care?

Fall on the lake would be ample time for Meghan to find answers to all these family questions. This smiling woman, her grandmother, deserved it. So did Sally, Meghan's mother.

Meghan just kept wondering why.

CHAPTER 20

Alan Shepard High School:
A Natural Reaction

October 2014

E d wondered if he'd ever finish sorting and discarding. It wasn't just birdhouse material that he had accumulated, but shelves of school materials. Boxes of folders on improving test scores, filing cabinets of curriculum design, articles on improving staff moral were all poured into cardboard boxes to be discarded. His den felt spacious, bare of its contents. He pulled off his outer shirt to cool himself. It was his tenth trip to the Outback, which was almost full. Stopping, he noticed that someone had left him a message on his phone while he was outside loading the SUV.

"Ed, this is Arlene Devoto over at Alan Shepard High. Look, I found a box of items in the hall closet outside your old office and thought you might want them. If you could come by to pick it up, that would be great. Hope all is well with your retirement. Such a great celebration the other night." There was a pause. "Oh, I almost forgot. If you have any extra keys to the building, we could use them," Arlene went on. "I'll leave the box right outside the main office for you. Thanks."

Ed sat down on the edge of his now-empty desk and sighed. His company had all left, and the camp seemed eerily quiet. The chat with Ted had lifted some of the burden of the secret he had been harboring for over quite a few weeks. His time in California brought back that sense of liberation he had not really enjoyed in years. Ed wanted to close doors so that new ones could truly open for him. He reached inside the pocket of his cargo shorts and pulled out a keychain.

Sure enough, there remained one lingering key on it that fit the back door of the high school. He needed to turn it in. Best to go over tonight, pick up the last remaining personality he'd forgotten, and leave the key. A pit formed in his stomach. He decided to go over right after dinner.

"Another piece of the past," he said aloud. "Another chapter closed."

*   *   *

Max paced around on the bedroom floor watching Meghan pull on and pull off three pairs of slacks. Another top was added to the pile on the bed. He headed toward the door and turned back to look at his restless owner. She walked back and forth before a full-length mirror, eyeing herself from different angles. Just as Max decided to stop and lay down, she nudged him away as she pulled out the sixth top from the bureau drawer. She moaned and shoved the drawer back in place.

Tonight, the organizational meeting for the 1974 class reunion was being held, and she was pretty sure that Sam Norton would be there. Many former students were also included in the list of emailed names she had perused before getting dressed. She wondered how much older she looked. Of course, they all would be older too.

"It's just a meeting," she reprimanded herself. "There is no reason for all this."

Her reflection stared back. It seemed to disagree.

Finally, glancing at the clock, she settled for a slim-fitting pair of jeans, a rust-colored cotton cowl-neck sweater, and gold accessories. The golden hoops gave her outfit a fall look and her brass cuffs set it all off without looking overdressed.

Pulling her hair up in a clasp and grabbing her corduroy jacket, the one with the leather elbow patches, she felt stylish and casual. The evenings on the lake were dropping into the forties and the extra layer would be needed later.

Max headed for the porch door.

"No. Not tonight, Max," Meghan warned. "I'll have to make my own impression this time."

Thoughts of the last encounter between Max and Sam's girlfriend still drew a grin from her lips.

She had briefly spoken to her neighbors, Bob and Alice, since they returned. They knew she was out for the night and had already agreed to keep an eye on the dog.

In minutes, Meghan was in the truck and on her way to the meeting. The drive helped settle her giddiness. She planned to act friendly and casual. Did it matter that Sam and Suzy were no longer engaged? Weren't these all just leftover emotions anyway? No reason to make it awkward when it was about a class reunion, not about her and Sam. In fact, the setting might finally settle once and for all the way she and Sam related now. She sat up straight, and looked at her own face in the rearview mirror; she gave her reflection a firm command.

"Tonight, present replaces past. Nothing more. Nothing less," she said aloud.

Twenty minutes later, Meghan pulled the red truck into the parking lot of the school. The shortened days were evident in the glow that emanated from the windows. The second floor was flooded with light where organizers were meeting in the school cafeteria. As if out of habit, Meghan glanced over at the room where she had taught English that one year, forty years ago. But she was not going there tonight.

The dashboard read 7:10. The meeting was set to begin at 7:00. Practically skipping up the steep granite stairs, Meghan opened the tall oak doors and soon passed the darkened offices of the nurse, guidance counselors and receptionist station. She knew her way to the cafeteria, teachers' lounge and down the hall to the auditorium. She cut off and took a left toward the lighted dining hall just off the southwest corner of the building. A gathering of about two dozen chatting people greeted her. Immediately, one called out to her.

"Miz Mac," a female voice sang out.

A tall brunette woman approached Meghan. She didn't recognize the woman at first, but suddenly it dawned on her who it was.

"Diane D'Angelo, so nice to see you." Meghan reached out her right hand.

Diane's face lit up.

"You look great, Mizzy Mac," she bubbled with enthusiasm. "Come on in. You can sit right next to Mister Norton."

Sam rose to slide over on the cafeteria bench, making room for Meghan to sit beside him. He nodded and continued to talk to another student about the difficulties arising from locating former classmates.

"So many have relocated to other parts of the country. Parents are our best resource. With girls changing names after marriage, it's easier to find the male members of the class," Sam was saying.

For the next twenty minutes, Meghan took notes on the margins of some scrap paper she'd found on the long table. She nodded, listened, and tried to stay focused on the various aspects of the event that would need to be planned. She breathed deeply and made it a point to try to identify every face before her. Many nodded and smiled back, apparently delighted that she had come.

There would be a decorating committee, a group to do advertising, another few to act as the liaison for the community. Someone needed to make an effort to reach every class member. Internet was their best bet, but also, the local newspaper and radio station could run a few ads. Meghan hadn't contributed anything except a grunt and vote on the many decisions, until suddenly, she was aware that all eyes were on her. She had been so focused on being calm, she had been caught not being present.

"We'll go get one," Sam was offering. "Come with me."

Before she knew what she had agreed to do, Meghan and Sam were heading down the dark halls toward the main office to find a copy of the 1974 yearbook.

"I spotted Al Dupont, the janitor, waxing floors," Sam was explaining. "He has the keys to all the doors. We need to unlock the door first and make sure we don't set off any alarms. Al was a client of mine. I helped him buy his house."

Meghan followed Sam.

"Isn't it weird being back here?" Sam commented while looking directly at Meghan.

"The place feels smaller, doesn't it?" she responded.

They had reached the intersection of the second floor and the stairwell leading up to the floor where they had taught together. Sam winked at Meghan.

"Let's go upstairs," he invited.

It wasn't a question. Meghan ran beside him up into the half-lit hallways leading to rooms 204 and 206. Stopping outside the classrooms, Sam and Meghan cupped their hands and peered into the room where sinks and lab desks could be seen.

"I can make out the chemical closet," Sam pointed out.

"Look, there's Old Lewy, the plastic human skeleton," Meghan added with a giggle.

For a few seconds, the two stood side by side and stared inside the room. Meghan stepped back and moved toward the adjacent room.

"There's the shelf where we kept our own set of encyclopedias. We had that tome of a dictionary and most of the classics. It was a private library between our Science and English rooms. I loved that old oak desk. It's still there. So many drawers."

Sam moved next to her and gazed inside. No one moved.

As they headed back down the hall, there was a quietness between them. Soon, they were back on the first floor and heading toward their intended destination: the main office. Sam spotted a light nearby, and headed down to pick up the keys from the janitor.

"Be right back."

The shadow of Sam's back left Meghan standing in darkness outside the main office doors. The thought of Ed Shea came to her at that minute. From here she could just make out the door to his former office.

It took only minutes for Sam to find Al and retrieve the keys. He jangled them musically toward Meghan, and then quickly inserted one into the metal door.

"This is the one. Al says the alarms are temporarily shut off. Something about installing a new system. Here we are," Sam announced as the door gave way.

The light switch for the office was another story. Neither of them knew which wall it was on. It took a few tries and a few moans as they bumped into the corners of metal desks and filing cabinets. Laughter sounded from the darkness.

"Damn," Sam shouted. "Can't see anything."

"It's got to be over by the coffee maker," Meghan offered.

Gradually, both their eyes adjusted to the dimly lit room. They went in opposite directions and circled the perimeter of the room, hands running along the walls. A red light above the hallway gave the room a crimson glow. Just as they reached the doorframe leading to the principal's waiting area, their hands met. They both hit the switch at the same time. The light came on. They could clearly see the shelf full of school yearbooks behind the receptionist's desk. Sam leaned forward and grabbed the one with "1974" engraved in golden on its spine.

Without missing a beat, he grabbed the book, leaned over and switched off the light. He pulled Meghan to himself. His lips found hers and held them. Meghan reached for the switch and turned it back on. She just stared at him.

"Déjà vu," Sam whispered into her ear.

"We need to get back," Meghan replied softly.

Sam smiled. He held up the yearbook in one hand and the keys in the other.

"I'll run these back to Al."

He bit his lip and disappeared down the dark hall, leaving Meghan breathlessly leaning against the cement walls of the hall.

Meghan glanced down the intersection of the two halls, the one Sam had just vanished into and the one that led to the red "Exit" sign just beyond the main office. Was it her imagination or had something just moved? The heavy fire door leading to the parking lot slammed shut, but not before Meghan made out the outline of a man leaving the building. He carried a box and had turned quickly when she came around the corner of the hall. A pit formed in her stomach. *No kidding. Déjà vu*, she thought. She knew the silhouette of that figure. It was Ed Shea.

She turned to see Sam coming up the opposite hall. They headed down to rejoin the reunion committee. When they reached the gathering, many of the members were folding up their chairs and saying their good-byes. Jimmy Norris, who had said little to Meghan all night, approached Sam and thanked him for delivering the yearbook.

"Mine was lost years ago. It may have burned in a fire," Jimmy admitted. He noticed how flushed Meghan's face was and that Sam seemed out of breath, but he said nothing. "Look, we plan to meet again to call people, email many, and send postcards out. I'll email both of you next week. This was a very productive meeting. A lot of those attending have kept in touch with their classmates and can get in touch with them easily." Jimmy nodded his head to affirm.

Sam and Meghan found themselves the last to leave. They pushed their benches against the dining-hall wall and headed for the front door.

"You always run away," Sam began. "I'd really like to take you out for dinner."

Meghan knew it was time to define what she and Sam were, but seeing Ed Shea leaving the school just minutes after the unexpected kiss left her feeling oddly confused.

"I'll give you a call next week," Sam said softly, as he opened the door to the red truck.

"My daughter, Ann, is supposed to come for a visit, so that would work," Meghan said slowly.

Sam leaned against the open door and pulled Meghan closer. He kissed her long and gently. Her knees felt like spaghetti. Her arms found his back. She held him close, and then stepped back. They just looked at one another for a second. Then Meghan crawled up into the cab of the truck, and Sam closed the door behind her.

"Goodnight, Sam," she called out as he stood on the curb watching her drive away. "See you soon."

CHAPTER 21

The Runes

October 2014

"Ed won't be coming over tonight," Bob yelled up to Alice as he headed down to the boat house. "He has to go over to the school to pick up some stuff he left."

Max could be seen at Bob's heels following closely behind. Alice wondered if the dog sensed the sadness in Bob since the death of his college friend Wally. She was looking forward to a visit from Ed to get her husband's mind off the tragedy. Wally's friendship dated back even further than the ones Bob had here on the lake; it went back before she and Bob had met.

She picked up her knitting again. Her hands hooped and dropped, and her mind followed the pattern. Since getting back from Florida, she certainly took notice of the cooler temperatures and felt the urge to make some winter scarves. This one was for Meghan who had been on her mind all day. Alice knew that tonight was the organizational meeting for the upcoming class of 1974, and that was haunting her thoughts. Meghan and she hadn't really had time to chat when she'd asked if Max could stay with them while she attended. The red truck was still missing.

Bob returned to the kitchen about thirty minutes later. Alice could hear him scrounging around in the refrigerator for a cold drink. Max slurped at his water bowl. She'd made quite a bit of progress on her knitting. Luckily the pattern didn't require much concentration, because she kept glancing over to see if her neighbor had returned.

Suddenly, Alice stored her knitting inside the quilted bag, and headed for the bedroom. Max took notice and followed her. As she passed through the kitchen, she reached into the towel drawers and withdrew something. It might be a good time to use these, she had decided. She would offer her services to Meghan.

The distinct sound of crunching stone reached Alice's attentive ears. Grabbing her fleece vest and stuffing her small package inside the front pocket, she called to Max.

"I'll walk Max over to the MacNamaras," Alice announced quickly to Bob. "I won't be long."

Bob looked up from the late-evening news and nodded absently as Max and Alice slipped out the front door.

Alice and company waited as Meghan parked the truck and ascended the porch steps. Before Meghan could turn on the inside lights, a figure emerged from the edge of the property.

"Hey, there. Thought I'd deliver your roommate," Alice called out as she approached the camp. Max whined.

Meghan jumped, her thoughts far away. Then she smiled at the sight of Alice. Max bound up on the porch, pushing his way inside. Alice followed.

"Hi. You're up late," Meghan muttered. "We missed you both at the retirement party."

Alice sauntered inside and sat expectantly on the couch. Meghan looked disheveled. She smiled broadly at her neighbor.

"I'm so sorry about Bob's friend. How is he doing?" Meghan figured that Alice might want to sit a bit.

Alice moved to the edge of the couch, both hands tucked inside the front of her fleece vest. Then she rose and sat stiffly at the kitchen table.

"Want a drink?" Meghan offered.

"Do I need one?" Alice smiled.

Meghan stopped and stared hard. What did she mean by that? What was the reason for this late-night visit when Max could have easily stayed over with them?

"Well, maybe," Meghan said. She pulled out two wine glasses and twisted the top off a cold bottle of wine. Slowly, Meghan poured them both a glass, still wondering what was on Alice's mind.

They both took a sip while Max stretched out in front of the camp door. Meghan sat down opposite Alice and sighed. Alice gave her friend a minute and then continued.

"So, I can read a face. Yours says something transpired. It's still flushed." Alice chuckled.

Meghan had had plenty of time on the ride home to review the details of the evening. Her insides had finally settled down. She had stopped sweating. But her tendency to blush, and the events of the meeting, had left her pink in the face. It was something hard to disguise.

"How about I ask you some questions and you decide which ones you want to answer?" Alice continued.

"Fair enough."

"Was Sam Norton there? And . . . did you have some time alone?"

"Yes, to both."

"Did you have the time to talk?"

"Yes and no."

Alice rolled her eyes. She would have to take another approach. She took a long sip of her drink and leaned across the table toward Meghan.

Suddenly, words started to pour out of Meghan. In choppy details, she related the twists and turns that led her to her rendezvous with Sam. "We went off to get the 1974 yearbook. They are kept in the main office. Of course, there were no lights on. We stumbled and laughed, met at the light switch and he kissed me. He walked me to the truck and we kissed again." Meghan's voice was soft.

Alice didn't interrupt.

"But there's a glitch," Meghan added.

Again, Alice waited, not wanting to stop the narrative.

Meghan stood up as if to walk away. She sat down again and gave Alice a look of exasperation. She was silent for a full minute.

"I think I know," Alice offered before Meghan could go on. "Ed was there."

Meghan looked across the table in disbelief. "How could you possibly know?" She rested her head on her folded arms.

"Psychic, right?" Alice smiled knowingly. "Not really. I just now put two and two together and figured out where both of you were tonight."

They sat for a minute. Meghan peeked up from her folded arms and shut both eyes.

"Did Ed see you?" Alice had to ask the obvious.

"Honestly? I don't know," Meghan admitted sheepishly.

The room was silent except for the soft snoring of Max. Meghan retrieved the bottle of wine and refilled both glasses. She sat down and stared at her friend. Alice pushed her right hand inside the front of her vest and withdrew a thick pack of purple cards.

"It was so impulsive. We were just enjoying the moment and all the memories the building held for us. We went upstairs to peek inside our old classrooms. His kiss felt so natural, like it did years before. But if Ed saw . . . anything, how do I explain it?" Meghan's voice trailed off.

Alice sat and let Meghan finish.

"Meghan, sometimes I do something for my closest friends when they are in some kind of transition. I consult the Rune Cards. They are an old Viking tradition, handed down from signs once carved on houses and rocks and even drawn on weapons of war. They have been translated onto small stones that readers carried in pouches, and finally the rune came to be depicted onto these cards." She tried to make her little speech short and to the point.

Meghan looked doubtful.

"I am not psychic. I cannot tell you the future or what you should do. I offer you messages that you must define for yourself. The meaning is something you alone can decipher. I just do a card spread and explain what the symbols and signs offer for your consideration."

Meghan looked down at the pack of strange cards, and then up at the honest face of her neighbor.

"Are they like Tarot cards?" Meghan wondered.

"No. They are far less associated with controversy. Often, Celtic woman used to read tea leaves. These cards are similar in that they present you with possibilities, not forecasts."

Meghan had gone with women friends at various times to consult palm readers and fortune tellers. The culture of Arizona offered more opportunities to experience such things. Many there believed in the power of certain gem stones, and many carried them to increase luck, health, or strength. She was open to such beliefs, but didn't practice any regularly. She likened much of this to rabbit feet, shamrocks or lucky horseshoes. And being of Irish descent, her own mother had exposed her to some superstitions. But the Rune cards were new to her.

Meghan had had quite an evening. The visit from such a trusted friend on such a night seemed fortuitous. She took a deep breath and looked at Alice's hands.

"Let's have a try," Meghan whispered. She got up to sit next to her friend, carrying the wine bottle with her.

CHAPTER 22

In the Cards

October 2014

A lice continued to explain the history of the Viking Runes. She explained that her cards were an artistic representation of twenty-five symbols and that their use was personal. No one could predict what was not yet in form, but sometimes, it was wise to look at a situation from another perspective. The use of these cards might draw her own insight into a clearer understanding of what was happening in her life. The more Alice described how the cards worked, the more intrigued Meghan became. The wine, the lateness, and the situation led her to be very open to suggestions. Perhaps, that was Alice's intent.

Alice placed the cards in Meghan's hands and instructed her to shuffle them. Then she took the pile and spread them face down in a large fan on the table.

"We will do a five-card spread. Select any five," Alice instructed.

Meghan randomly slid five cards from the pack before her. Alice turned them over one by one.

"The cards to your left represent what had happened. The cards to the right symbolize more of the possibilities. Altogether, they are a flow of events in which you find yourself. Think about this as I translate what each sign represents. Apply them loosely to your dilemma."

The five cards read: Warrior, Fertility, Constraint, Self and Possessions

In a soft voice, Alice instructed Meghan to hold her quandary in her mind. She reinforced the importance of being open to the spread's message.

"Let the words guide you," Alice reminded her friend. "The Warrior card reminds you to be innocent and trusting, not too attached to reaching a quick solution. Its message is to stay out of your own way, be patient, and persevere. A soldier must not rush into battle. Many warriors wore this symbol on their shield when going into battle."

Meghan sat and stared at the colorful image on the card.

"The second card in your spread, Fertility, points out that a new life is unfolding. You must give up old ways for something new to enter. Something must be resolved first, however. That completion is your first task."

Meghan stared at the image of a butterfly coming out of its closed chrysalis state and felt like the image of the transposed child, on the verge of something new and different happening.

"Your third card, Constraint, is a very introspective card. It asks that you question why you stop yourself from acting. What is it that keeps you at bay? Is there a lesson you have not yet learned? Every adversity is there to teach you. They too are your guides."

Meghan reached for her wine. The glass was empty. She stared at the remaining two cards. She did not decipher any of the messages out loud, nor did Alice add any of her own. A cool breeze floated in through the open window. The smell of water and fall filled the room. Max rose and relocated under the table, leaning his nose against Meghan's feet.

"The fourth card speaks more to the future. And the one you selected is the card of Self. This is a water sign, fluid and deep. Allow things to flow. Know yourself before you choose. All real answers rise from your heart," Alice added.

Meghan was entranced. She felt calmer than she had felt all evening. Alice's voice remained even and low. She did not explain how any of this pertained to Meghan, but let the words seep in naturally.

"Seeds must grow in their own way."

Meghan nodded

"This is the final card in you spread. It is the card of Possessions. It represents choice. It is in a reverse position, which adds strength to its message."

Meghan noticed that the card was upside down.

"This last card in your spread reminds you to consider what you most value. Something is usually lost when we gain. Some things fade out while other things abide. You must choose what is truly worthy and what will endure."

Alice allowed Meghan to glance once more across the five-card spread before them. Then she gathered up the cards and shuffled them back into the pack. She noticed that Meghan's eyes were far away. She was confident that Meghan had received the advice she needed, that something rang true to her.

Alice started to get up to leave. It had to be one in the morning. She had accomplished her mission, to connect with her friend and to offer some wise advice. She hoped the cards left her friend peaceful.

"It's late," Alice said softly. "Think about all that you heard. Let it settle in your mind and heart. Apply it to your own life. We can talk another time."

Meghan didn't move. Alice sat down again. As if an afterthought, she handed the pack to Meghan.

"Cut the pack," she directed.

Meghan shuffled, placed the entire set before her, and lifted about half. Alice turned the exposed card up: Signals   Alice smiled.

"This card, Signals, instills in the receiver a reminder to be aware of messages you receive. There will be gifts that guide you. Some of it may not be welcome; accept it as well. Be aware of chance meetings. New lives begin with new encounters with those wiser than yourself."

With teary eyes, Meghan gave her friend a hug. Alice slipped out the door and headed quietly back to her own camp.

It took Meghan only minutes to take off her clothes and slip into bed. She could feel the soft kiss of Sam still lingering on her lips, and the easy, gentle voice of Alice, as she drifted off to sleep.

So many signs. So much to consider.

CHAPTER 23

Holiday Visitor

October 14–15, 2014

Annie knew that her mother had been up the night before and had attended an organizational meeting for a reunion for Alan Shepard High School. In her mother's other life, before the advent of motherhood, she knew that Meghan had had a stint at teaching there. It did seem odd that she felt such a connection to the year 1974, but if it helped her mother settle in for the fall, she figured that such community involvement was a positive thing. She had told her mother that she was in the area for a teachers' seminar and would come by the lake. She had arrived earlier than expected and didn't want to wake Meghan.

Max wasted no time in announcing that someone was on the grounds. Despite Annie's effort to sneak down to the beach, he was there in moments. He started to bark.

"Quiet," she whispered to him. "Come sit," she directed him.

He recognized her and, after much wiggling and pawing, sat next to her on the damp beach sand.

Mist rose from the early morning surface of Pawtuckaway Lake. Annie put an arm around Max's ample back, and the two sat companionably looking out over the calm surface. It was cooler than it had been her last visit. She had broken off with her boyfriend since then, and although she still had moments of sadness, the time between then and now had been a busy one. Once school reconvened, she involved herself in the new school year. The Columbus Day holiday always offered her a nice break. This workshop, held in Portsmouth, just northeast of the lake, offered her the perfect opportunity to extend her time off and visit with her mother.

It was about seven in the morning. Annie pulled her sweater tighter around her neck. She didn't want to go inside, yet. She assumed that Meghan was still asleep, but she was not.

Inside, Meghan lay awake trying to compose both herself and her thoughts surrounding the previous evening's happenings. Her observant daughter would detect any odd behavior shown by her mother. Thoughts around Sam or Ed would have to be sorted out later, after her daughter's visit. One of her rules as a parent was to tend to her family first, compartmentalizing any other concerns for their own time. She would talk to Sam later in the week, and worrying about it would change nothing. She threw back the bed covers and grabbed her well-worn sweatshirt from the chair beside the night table. Time to welcome the visitor she knew had arrived. Luckily, Max had acted as temporary host.

Meghan headed for the kitchen to brew some coffee and to greet the day. Other things could wait. She looked out the front window just as Annie rose from her sandy seat, followed by Max.

"Good morning," Annie yelled up to her mother.

Meghan waved them inside, and pulled two chairs out on the porch. The aroma of coffee soon filled the morning air.

* * *

Alice too had risen early. She hoped her card readings had not upset Meghan. Often, in her experience, the recipients of her Rune messages wanted to talk more after they had time to digest what the signs implied. She noticed that Annie had arrived; this put a damper on further discussion.

Bob stumbled half-awake into the kitchen where Alice sipped ginger lemon tea.

"You're up early," he commented. "Company arrive next door?"

He lifted his chin ever so slightly in the direction of the MacNamara camp.

"Yes. Annie is there for a few days."

"Good," Bob stated with a certain defiance. "Maybe things will cool down a bit."

Alice refused to react to his comment. She had avoided any discussion concerning the reunion meeting but couldn't help wondering what he already knew. He and Ed emailed sometimes, but she respected his privacy. Had Ed already gotten in touch with her husband?

"You got to bed rather late after delivering Max to Meghan, is all . . ." Bob didn't finish his thoughts. He was aware of what he referred to as his wife's gypsy side and seemed to have already assumed that more than idle chatter had kept Alice at her neighbor's so late.

Rolling her eyes and picking up her unfinished knitting, Alice just shrugged. "Women need women talk sometimes," she stated matter-of-factly.

Bob's face took on a brief expression of concern, but he turned quickly before he thought Alice had noticed it. He directed a crooked smile her way, and then he headed down the hall, leaving his wife to wonder what he was aware of but chose to keep to himself.

113

Alice realized her hands were gripping her knitting needles too tightly and she consciously made an effort to loosen them. A looser knit felt better around the neck and she preferred space in her pieces. Like her attitude about life, Allice didn't want to be intrusive, but part of her hoped that Meghan would call upon her again. She would avail herself, but only if asked.

Clearly, the fabric of life was getting into a very tangled mess indeed. She pulled at her work to allow the weave more room to breathe.

CHAPTER 24

Distractions

October 14, 2014

To Meghan's relief, Annie's short visit didn't involve any heart-to-heart chats. Her daughter merely wanted to extend her conference days before returning to work. Meghan did notice that the unruly hair and darkly circled eyes were absent, and that her daughter seemed to have moved on from her heartbreak. The former boyfriend's name never came up.

The two women enjoyed a cruise out on the lake, lounging around reading and tossing balls to the only male in the house — Max. Annie even ventured into the lake for a swim, as if determined to steal one last snippet of summer. Her dip was followed by a very hot shower and a much-appreciated cup of steaming hot chocolate provided by her mother.

Conversations centered primarily around Annie's upcoming classes, the variety of students she had been given and lesson plans she hoped to implement that the recent workshop had inspired. Meghan remembered how such teacher getaways had always enriched her. Ed Shea had been instrumental in signing her up. She carefully veered away from sharing her own memories in the classroom for fear of being derailed and talking about Sam. Fortunately for Meghan, the visit was brief, and she was able to avoid what was simmering on her own back burner — Sam Norton.

"There is a new history teacher at school," Annie mentioned. "He taught in Boston and is from Maine. We have the same duty in the cafeteria and have been able to get to know one another. He is single."

"That sounds like it has possibilities," Meghan responded with a warm smile.

Annie seemed to take no notice that her mother had little else to add. This was her usual response, so no red flags went up. The conversations were light and chatty.

"Will we spend Thanksgiving here at Pawtuckaway Lake?" Annie inquired as she and Meghan spent the evening snuggled under quilts and watching their favorite movie: *Under the Tuscan Sun*. Meghan realized just how hard she had been focusing on not divulging anything of the turmoil she held at bay, and had had to pause to let the question register.

"Well, that seems to be the logical thing. Arizona is out. This kitchen is too small to prepare the usual feast, but there are pre-cooked turkeys. And we could do a kind of pot luck."

Annie had her own thoughts as to who might attend, as did Meghan. But neither mentioned it. The event was still weeks away.

Annie's overnight was over too quickly, and Meghan tried not to feel the immediate absence when she woke up to see her only daughter off at five the following morning. Max sensed the mood and seemed to stick closely to Annie as she dressed in work clothes, taking extra care with her hair and make-up. Time on the lake was never long enough.

Meghan had poured hazelnut coffee into a Styrofoam cup for Annie to take with her. She added an orange, already sectioned, and packed it inside a plastic sandwich bag. Meghan dropped in one of her summer floral colored napkins and a note too.

The stationery depicted two Adirondack chairs perched by a shore, the sun shining brightly over water in the background. She had written:

"Honey,

Remember, the heart is always ready to love. The lake
is our place to heal. And you are a MacNamara. Be true
to yourself.

Love,

Mom."

Later in the day, when Annie would be miles down the road, Meghan
would feel that she had given her daughter what she needed: assurance,
attention, and freedom to choose.

Meghan stood with Max and waved as Annie shut the door on her
white Honda and pulled out of the driveway. A hand waved out the driver's
window. Meghan's eyes misted over. She was at her own crossroads and
thought no one really knew it. She had to give Sam an answer. He was next
on her agenda. She couldn't seem to visualize the outcome and felt isolated
in her own world. Without a thought, she gave Max a pat. He glanced up
and they headed into the empty camp together.

A curtain was adjusted in the bedroom at the Finches' next door.
Alice had been up to see the white Honda depart. She knew that her friend's
heart was in turmoil, but all she could do now was wait and see.

*   *   *

Annie needed gas and stopped at the nearest gas station to fill up.
She took a sip of the still-hot coffee and reached in for the soft item she felt
tucked inside the brown paper bag. As she pulled out the napkin, a note
fell to the floor.

"What's this?" she said aloud as she reached down to retrieve it.

Opening it, she wondered what was so important. The note was not
her mother's normal act. As she read the short blessing, she admitted that
Meghan had seemed quieter than usual. She hadn't given it much thought

earlier, but now she let it slip into her consciousness. What was it that the lake did to them all? So thoughtful. And why did her mother feel the need to write it down instead of just saying it? The MacNamaras were kind to each other, but not so expressive as this.

The trip to the lake was only a distraction for Annie. The school year was off to a good start, and she felt sure that her own life was on the right track. But what was going on with her mother? Was she sick? Would she not reveal it? Suddenly, Annie felt a tinge of selfishness. She hadn't really focused on her mother at all. Had she missed something important? Who would know?

Placing the card inside her school bag, Annie pumped the gas and cleaned her windshields. But her mind was back at the empty camp. She needed to find out more. She felt she was missing something that her mother wasn't ready to share. And she already knew whom to ask.

CHAPTER 25

Recipes of Love

October 15, 2014

There was a short window of time for Meghan to fall into after Annie had left, and she did. With no one to take her mind off the looming date, Meghan's mind ran two images, sometimes superimposed on one another, but other times colliding like ongoing trains on the same track. Ed Shea and Sam Norton were those trains. With all the self-discipline she could muster, she focused on the months ahead. She wondered what Alice might contribute, but was afraid to ask.

Columbus Day had proven to be more like Columbus Week. Had the explorer ever dreamed when he set foot in the new world that someday the settlers would sit down and eat with the natives? Or was he more worried about surviving the dangers of ocean travel with only sails and stars to carry him? Meghan wanted to plan the holiday of Thanksgiving, but instead, her mind was on Rune cards and mysterious messages and the turmoil in her own heart. Where was her journey taking her? What was in the stars for her?

She and Max sat under the old pine tree near the dock. She mixed the honey she had taken to adding to her morning tea, and looked out over the purple surface of the lake. Annie had left her room spotless. She had forgotten nothing and had not called about the note. Meghan wanted only to reassure her daughter, and hoped she had not given Annie any reason to worry. Annie was a capable young woman and free to give her heart to someone else. Was she?

The Finch household appeared empty. Alice's car was missing. She was probably off at the library where she volunteered a few hours a week. Good thing, because it would have been hard not to go over and discuss the late-night revelations of the strange card-reading Alice had done for her. Suddenly, Max shot off after a squirrel he had been observing. It ran up a tree leaving him gazing up in frustration.

"Too fast, huh?" she teased. "Thanksgiving is only weeks away. It will be hard to put together much in such cramped quarters," she said aloud. She pictured her own spacious kitchen in Arizona, with her dual ovens and enormous oak table. "That isn't here. If the MacNamaras managed to pull together a nice family gathering in the past, so can I," she told herself firmly.

She needed the celebration to be simple, satisfying and yet traditional in the most essential way. How was she to do that without some king of menu? Sally wasn't there to help.

Slouching inside the old Irish knit sweater she had gotten in the habit of wearing, she took a long sip of her tea. The liquid smelled wonderful as the warm sugary taste of honey made its way down her throat. A thought suddenly came to her mind; she sat up straight and choked. Coughing, she jumped up. She had a solution. Max followed.

There was an old recipe box under the kitchen sink, behind bottles of dish soap, Brillo pads, Ajax dispensers, ammonia, and Pine Sol. That might hold the magic touch she needed to resurrect the kind of food most fitting for a family feast.

Max ran up and sat beside her. His food was also stored in the same cabinet. He sat and gave her the doe-eyed look that every puppy masters. She gave him a direct stare.

"Later, old fellow. You just ate!"

The cleaning bottles piled up on the floor as Meghan removed two dish pans and a rubber strainer. A new pack of sponges in rainbow colors fell to the floor. She remembered finding the tin box and returning it to the back of the shelf. Finally, her hand hit the metal surface and she withdrew the item to the front of the cabinet. Its familiar shape caused her to pause. She opened the top slowly as if it held golden treasures. It might just make Thanksgiving old-fashioned, if not gourmet.

Opening the refrigerator, Meghan poured milk into a glass and headed out to the porch with her recipe tin in hand. She pulled on a thick pair of sweats and settled into the chair next to a maple two-leaf table. She flicked on the small table lamp for extra light. Max circled around three times before getting it just right, and then he settled on the rug near the porch door. His eyes focused on the Finches' camp.

The box itself had been repainted. From the chips along the edges, it might have been originally green. However, someone had put a coat of light cream paint on it and then proceeded to paint red strawberries, green vines, and yellow chickens on the top and sides. A squiggle-like design ran along the bottom of the front. The place where a latch might have been was decorated with miniature pineapples. The entire creation, though very original, resulted in a bohemian design, almost childlike in its varied colors and shapes.

There was no order to the collection of assorted recipes crammed inside: chicken soup, creamed corn, egg salad, cinnamon buns, and raspberry jam were among the first Meghan removed. She quickly recognized from her weeks of reading Sally's journal and Agnes' diaries that both women had contributed to the box's contents. Their different handwriting was evident among the contributions.

Rusted paper clips held the menus for special occasions: birthday cakes with jam and cream filling, Halloween cookies with marshmallow ghosts, whoopee pies for Christmas, cheese balls with walnuts for New Year's Eve and punch with orange sherbet for showers. Like her photos, the recipes told a story about family, traditions, and important occasions, and almost automatically, Meghan began to organize and categorize the various concoctions. The contents of the metal box made neat little piles on the porch table. Meghan found herself once more visiting the households and lives of the ladies of the MacNamara clan.

Like an alarm to awaken her from her sojourn into the past, the phone buzzed, and Meghan got up to answer it. She felt startled and half-expected her own mother to be on the other end. She assumed it was Annie just calling to thank her for the visit and was prepared to tell her about the contents of the tin, but the voice she heard was clearly male.

"Hey, how about dinner tonight?" he asked.

Meghan held the receiver tightly. She stared at the emptied recipe box and slowly closed the lid. Was it already time to answer some of her own questions? The voice waited for her to speak. Had that time arrived?

CHAPTER 26

Words from the Past

1936

M eghan paused, cleared her throat, and found her voice. "Hello." It sounded as if she had just woken up.

"Hi. It's me, Kevin. Were you sleeping?" the male voice asked.

She placed her left hand stiffly on the arm of the couch, her right hand gripping the phone as if it would keep her afloat. Taking a deep breath, Meghan consciously forced her shoulders to drop. She closed her eyes. "Oh, Hi Kevin. So good to hear from you. What's up?"

A few minutes earlier, Annie had called Kevin, her brother, from the teachers' room immediately after the sound of the homeroom bell had rung. She had a free period, the staff room was empty and she made the call as brief as she could, not wanting to raise unnecessary concern.

"Why not give Mom a quick call? Just to check in. She isn't acting herself." Annie hesitated. She had reached her brother on his cellphone, and seeing her number, he had picked up quickly. She didn't call often.

"You know, I can do better. I'm up here in Boston on business, as it happens. I will drive up," he said with conviction.

Annie already felt better. She could get another person's perspective.

"It's probably nothing, but she usually isn't so mushy. You know? Just in case," Annie added.

Meghan listened as Kevin explained why he happened to be in her neck of the woods, and how he would like to have dinner. It gave her a minute to compose herself. She was relieved that it had been him on the other end of the phone.

"I could be there around seven. Is that too late?" he asked.

"Not at all. It would be wonderful. I'll be ready."

Meghan could have hugged him for this unexpected visit. The *date* she was anticipating with Sam sometime next week could wait.

When she ended the call, she sat for a moment still in that trance she fell into when she spent time with the family archives. She knew she could find the perfect holiday menu among the collection inside the recipe tin. With Kevin coming, she could also explain how they might make it a pot luck feast and plan what Julie and the kids could bring up. Meghan began to picture festive paper plates, tablecloths and napkins for the occasion. It would be less clean-up with the use of some disposables. It was camp after all.

Returning to the recipes jammed inside the old box, Meghan picked up her mental game of guessing which ones were put there by Sally and which were Agnes'. At some point, Sally had stopped recording on recipe cards, and toward the middle of the box, Meghan discovered clippings of preprinted recipes cut from assorted magazines. The change in her parents' diet was reflected there too as her mother began to creatively use herbs and spices. These were newer additions at the back end of the colorful container.

The piles grew, and the old foldable television table was soon pulled up beside the porch table as an extension. This allowed Meghan to create yet another category: potpourri. These included odd mixtures of marinades made with mostly olive oil, lemon juice and herbs; chicken broiled with vegetables on the grill; egg-nog ice cream; and a special tuna salad made with cooked eggs, chives, and cucumbers.

The end of the metal container was almost in sight. There was one last set of cards that looked to belong to Agnes; they were yellowed and held firmly with a dried and crumbled rubber band. The band began to disintegrate as Meghan loosened the first card.

She stopped. Only the top card held a recipe. The others proved not to be recipe cards at all, but postcards. She peeled off the remaining sticky rubber from the edges of the first one. They depicted images of cities all over the East: Concord, Boston, New York, Portland, and Burlington. Each was addressed to Agnes. At the bottom appeared a simple letter "W." It was Wil MacNamara's correspondence. The dates were scattered throughout the 1930s.

Many of the postcards were interspersed with faded newspaper clippings. Taking a clean butter knife from the counter, Meghan wedged it in between to separate the cards from the news articles. They had been pressed together so long that the cards on the front had practically melted into the old news prints in between. The result resembled a ham and cheese sandwich.

Without looking away, Meghan pulled up the leaf on the oak table and attempted to display the postcards and news clippings together, looking for a pattern. The dates might help to close the gap she repeatedly found in both Sally's journals and Agnes' diary. These cards filled in the years between 1931 and 1936, when Agnes ceased to do regular entries, and Sally seemed lost as to what to write.

The notes on the back of each card repeatedly sent a positive message to the MacNamaras in Manchester. They reported Wil's whereabouts, what he had seen and what he was doing, and his ongoing theme was the desire to be home.

"Mar. 5, 1933

Arrived in NYC. Looks promising. FDR is our only hope. Miss you all.

Love, W."

Meghan placed the cards in order. Many of the news clippings seemed beyond repair. She retrieved her glasses from the table next to the couch, a set of tweezers from the bathroom and a sharp knife to aid her in peeling the multiple layers of paper apart. She took her time, feeling like an archaeologist sifting at a site.

A narrative of parallel lives laid out before her eyes: the one Wil had led on the railroad, and the other unfolding in one small place in the United States in the 1930s, Manchester, New Hampshire.

One article related the flood that hit the city in 1936 and the hurricane that followed in 1938. One showed a faded photo of a flooded Merrimac River, bridges collapsing, and streets flowing with water. One headlined the closing of the Amoskeag Mills. One small piece announced that the Manchester Board of Health had declared Pine Island Pond unsuitable for public swimming. Meghan thought this an odd thing to care about until she discovered a wrinkled photo folded inside.

In it, a very young couple stood together under a Ferris wheel. Pulling her glasses low on the bridge of her nose, Meghan studied the faces. They were, unmistakably, Sally and Jack. He looked about fifteen. Three lines were scrawled on the reverse side:

"Before the trees fell.
Our Honeymoon Express
1936"

The family story was taking yet another turn. How young were her parents when they began to show signs of attraction toward one another? Was this the first spark? Here they were standing together before an enormous Ferris wheel. Someone had caught the moment. She continued to read from the tin's collection.

The last article in the wad simply read:

> "December 25, 1936
> The Amoskeag Declares Bankruptcy."

With the collapse of the largest employer in the city of Manchester, it would be a Christmas no one would forget. Wil had no reason to return.

The last few postcards became very dispersed, the cities farther apart. The tale of Wil MacNamara's adventure on the rails left many months out. Was it up to Meghan to fill them in? Could she?

She found a plastic container with a water-proof top and placed the last of the recipe tin's contents inside. They would be safer there. The tale of Sally and Jack continued. The recipe tin seemed an unlikely place to put the information. Who had left them there? And where did this trail of Wil's lead?

Meghan stared out on the lake. So many hands had played a part in this reconstruction of the family story. Someone wanted the entire tale told. Was it leading to more sorrow? Were the missing pieces so vital? Did it matter in the end?

Pawtuckaway Lake sat dark and silent before her. She would continue to dive deeply. What would she find?

Autumn was certainly proving to be the season for her colorful family tale.

CHAPTER 27

Remembering Pine Island Park

1936

Emotions of confidence and care washed over Meghan as both of her children continued to visit the lake. Annie appeared to be starting the school year off in a good place, even admitting that there might be someone of interest in her life. And both of them were successfully keeping thoughts of Sam at bay for her. So far, Sam had not called.

Kevin's sudden offer to drive up and take her out to dinner was no doubt to celebrate her recent birthday on October 12. She had received the most adorable cards from her grandchildren: one card depicting a boy fishing from a small red boat, wearing an enormous life jacket. The inside message read: "Be safe but have fun on your Special day. Love, Tommy." Annie had left her a generous gift card to spend at the mall in Manchester. She envisioned some nice fall-colored clothes in her future.

Kevin drove up with the radio off. Annie's concern about their mother's health kept running through his mind. With his mother turning a year older, it wasn't beyond the possibility that her health should be taken into consideration. She was living alone on the lake. But it was the emotional message left inside her breakfast bag that had set his sister Annie wondering. She wanted him to call her after their dinner and report any findings. He hoped there were none.

It wasn't odd that he wanted to wish his mother on her birthday in person; his visit shouldn't set off any red flags. He didn't need any excuse to go to the lake, either. Like a lawyer, he was preparing his line of questioning to determine if she was guilty of keeping something from them. Was it serious?

Meghan planned to recommend that Kevin take her to Manchester to one of the restaurants she had noticed on a recent visit to South Willow Street. She missed her usual diet of Mexican fare. She had enjoyed it while living in Arizona. She'd suggest Cactus Jack's. With the colors of the West in her mind, she chose what to wear a long gauze skirt with a mixture of aqua, golden yellow and black, a long-sleeve black tee-shirt, her silver dangle earrings and cuffs and brown leather sandals. She was pushing the bare feet. Perhaps, some of her birthday money could go toward a nice pair of leather boots too.

Knowing that Kevin wasn't due for another two hours, Meghan found herself drawn back to the surprise addition she had discovered in the back of the old recipe box: the tiny photo of Sally and Jack standing in Pine Island Park and dated 1936. The postcards of Wil MacNamara's search for work in the thirties were helpful pieces to the ongoing puzzle that she was assembling. She had already placed that photo inside the old tome of a Webster's Dictionary, to flatten it. At the same time, her goal of holding a traditional Thanksgiving holiday at the lake continued to gnaw at her. Hadn't she remembered seeing some cook books among Jack's collection? She headed back behind his reading chair to retrace her steps.

Running her fingers over the bindings, Meghan tilted her head sideways to read the titles. Piled up at the far end of the second shelf were Sally's books. Magazines dating from the 1980s reflected Sally's growing interest in herbs. Corners of the periodicals peeked out from an uneven pile, many dog-eared. But this wasn't what Meghan was searching for today. She wanted old family favorites, and she felt certain that they would be among these shelves.

Sure enough, at the very bottom of Sally's culinary collection sat a dusty copy of a Betty Crocker cook book — a must for every bride. Many believed that it held the secrets to many successful marriages over the decades. What young housewife hadn't referred to it when learning how to place silverware for a formal dinner, to thicken gravy or simply to ensure the proper timing for a soft-boiled egg? She pulled it from its slot on the shelf.

This edition of Betty Crocker was dated 1961. Laying it on her lap, she settled into Jack's soft leather chair and turned to the section marked "Holiday." There she found the penciled-in marks made by Sally. Here was the recipe used for her cranberry-orange relish, and the added ingredients to her moist bread stuffing. It was just what Meghan would include in a few weeks at her own family Thanksgiving.

What about that photo she thought? What was she missing? Where could she find out about the park, the dates, and the reason the photo had been so carefully included among the postcard collection? What would her children suggest she do? Meghan was in the habit of doing her research in books. She did have a computer she could use.

So that was her next step. Turning it on, she typed in a search for "Pine Island Park, Manchester, New Hampshire," and waited. The computer immediately presented her with another screen and a list of articles about old trolley parks.

Max had wandered in and curled himself at her feet.

"Not bad for an old girl," she told him. "Look at this." She pointed to the screen. "Computer savvy," she boasted.

Scrolling down, she selected one of the articles and began to read. The pieces mentioned Pine Island along with another park in the state, Canobie Lake. She knew that the latter one was still open, having seen many ads for it at state rest areas along the highway. She had picked up a flyer and planned to take Tommy and Beth. But Meghan wanted to learn about the one off Calef Road in Manchester this time.

There it was. There was even a picture of the old signage.

Opened in 1902, Pine Island began as a small park offering a place to picnic, boat and swim. Apparently, thousands of local residents had visited it regularly. The Boston and Maine railroad would book the entire park for its company outings. Workers from the local wool, cotton, textile, and shoe factories enjoyed bringing their families. Fireworks regularly entertained those who came.

In 1908, a figure 8 roller coaster was added. That skeleton of a roller coaster remained, in Meghan's memory, years later.

Starting out as a place to visit at the end of the line, trains delivered passengers to the park for years. You could pick up a trolley on Elm Street in downtown Manchester, and be delivered to the park in under twenty minutes. The park was full of pine trees to sit under, providing cooling shade.

As usual, Meghan was easily distracted by the photos and comments that had been added about the park. It was the year 1936 that she was most curious about. The few words on the back of the photo had left her wanting to know more.

There it was, sure enough. In 1936, in addition to the Pine Island Pond being declared polluted, Mother Nature began her ongoing ravages to the park. The flood of the same year destroyed much of the safe waters around the city. A hurricane in 1938 destroyed an estimated three thousand of the park's grand old pine trees. Her parents had stood at the threshold of the old place. The note in Jack's handwriting had only said, "Before the trees fell." But what was the rest?

They had been photographed standing before a Ferris wheel that, as it turned out, was called "The Honeymoon Express." Jack was about fifteen at the time of the photo. There they stood on the threshold of adulthood, an age that would usher in hard times and economic disasters. Not just the park would fall into decay, but their childhood was quickly coming to an end as well.

Further reading revealed to Meghan why she was able to recall some aspects of the park herself. The place closed in 1962 when a fire engulfed much of the park. The carousel dating back to 1904 with its hand-carved horses was destroyed.

This moment captured in time had been saved. And who had stuck the image in a rusty recipe box? How long had it been hidden among the comfort food recipes of one Manchester family?

She sat back and closed her eyes. She could conjure up vague memories of some of the rides still functioning in the late 1950s. There were miniature boats that circled in water, teacups spinning on saucers and the haunting outline of the abandoned roller coaster. These images felt real to her. The rest she could only imagine from talk she had overheard from her parents.

Looking at the time on the computer screen, Meghan realized she needed to pull herself back and get ready for dinner with Kevin. She hit Save, clicked the Off button and headed for the bedroom.

While putting on her outfit, she wondered how many stories remained untold. This unusual twist only added to the tale of her family. The Pawtuckaway Lake house was the last vestige of memorabilia she had. If she was acting oddly, it may have been because this visit to the past felt as if the journey had been just waiting for her return.

This night was a celebration of her birthday. Jack had been born in October as well, on the eighth day. As much as Sally had retrieved of the family legacy, Jack seemed to have had his own way of hiding clues. There were multiple trails left, and Meghan was following them all.

With one foot in her own past and the other in the moment, Meghan faced herself in the mirror. Wil MacNamara remained the man in question. His story was still unfinished.

But couldn't this be said of her own?

CHAPTER 28

Only Heartsick

2014

Kevin walked with deliberate steps toward the camp door, unaware that his arrival had already been detected next door. Alice Finch was quick to see the car pull in bearing Connecticut plates. It was her time in the evening to relax and knit; she rocked slowly in her chair beside the bedroom window and watched him. She felt a bit nosy, but couldn't seem to help herself lately. Odd to have him visit mid-week. Alice hoped all was well.

Meghan also heard the crunch of stones beneath the car, and slid the photo taken at Pine Island Park back into the huge dictionary tome. This was dinner with her son, and her birthday. She wanted to discuss plans for Thanksgiving, and to enjoy Kevin's company free of other intruding thoughts.

Watching Kevin stride toward the camp, she was struck by how similar it was to Tom's. They both leaned forward as if anticipating what lay ahead. Neither looked up. It was a wonder that they didn't run into things. She smiled at the memory.

Kevin knocked on the door and let himself in. "Hey, Mom. Ready to eat?" he called out.

"Be right out."

He headed for the bathroom. They met up a few minutes later inside the front door.

Quickly, Kevin wrapped his arms around his mother. She felt solid. He placed a quick kiss on her forehead and looked quickly into her face. He saw no signs of impending sickness. They headed out the door and were driving toward Mountain Road in minutes.

"So where are we going?" Kevin inquired.

"How about Manchester? I am dying for tacos and salsa."

"Sound good to me." He headed west.

The drive took about thirty minutes. Kevin chatted about all that had transpired since their lake visit.

"Tommy is struggling with math. He can recite the PLU numbers on the produce Julie buys at the market. He will tell you many of the averages of the Boston Red Sox. How can it be that he has trouble with math?" Kevin asked incredulously.

Meghan was quick to defend her grandson. "Maybe, he's better with practical numbers. You know the calculations that are useful, like measuring a room or adding up totals. I hated abstract math. And many of my students used to complain, wondering when they would use all those formulas in real life."

Kevin looked over, amused at his mother's reasoning.

She had already broken her own promise not to discuss anything pertaining to her days at Alan Shepard. Sam Norton's students used to hate having to do chemical formulas in his classes, and metrics was foremost among their dislikes. Weren't inches and feet much easier to use? She pushed it all from her mind.

"How is Beth?" Meghan asked.

"She and Julie have been spending a lot of time together in the kitchen lately. She had quite a time frosting cupcakes last week. Julie also let her mix up the meatloaf with her bare hands. I think we have the makings of a chef," he said proudly.

Meghan interrupted periodically to give directions, but Kevin had an inherent good sense of direction. Like Tom, he seemed born with an inner compass.

"I am planning our menu for Thanksgiving. I found some of my mother's old favorites. I'll have to talk to Julie. I was thinking that she and Beth might cook up some special dish."

Kevin nodded in agreement.

They pulled into an appealing Mexican restaurant called CJ's. The outside café was closed due to cold evening temperatures, but a pitcher of sangria tasted just as good enjoyed inside. The conversation continued on about future visits, when their food arrived.

"So, how is everything going on the lake?" Kevin inquired. "How is Ed Shea?"

He dipped a large red corn chip into the salsa, dripping some on the front of his white shirt. Without hesitation, Meghan reached over with a napkin dipped into her water glass to clean it. They both laughed.

"Just being your mother," Meghan joked with a chuckle. "I am enjoying the cooler weather. I've joined a scrapbooking club. Ed's retirement gathering was a great success, with lots of my former students in attendance. He and your uncle Ted tried to spend as much time as they could together, but Ted only had two days."

The waiter had arrived to refill glasses with ice and check up on their meals. Meghan fidgeted with a corn chip and dipped pieces into the salsa. Kevin seemed not to notice her evasiveness about Ed.

He decided to go off in the direction he had come to investigate.

"So, Mom. Are you all set with a doctor, or flu shots or any other usual thing? You know, any medical emergency you might have? Max has a vet; how are you set?"

"Actually, I just had such a chat with Alice. She recommended her own doctor. I need to call to see if he takes new patients. I can get a flu shot at any drugstore. There is one right nearby," she said giving no indication that there was any cause for alarm.

The evening continued with Meghan discussing her plans to work on the 1974 reunion, her ongoing projects at the camp and her renewed acquaintance with people from Hampton Hills.

"How is your MacNamara exploration going? Any skeletons in the old family closet?" Kevin asked teasingly.

Meghan took a bite of her chicken taco and a sip of her sangria. "I've learned a lot about our family from all the pictures and notes. Your grandfather loved his family, but didn't like to talk much about his father Wil MacNamara. The Great Depression really took a toll on so many lives. Even Agnes seemed to have stopped mentioning him in her journal at one point."

"I thought Wil died of pneumonia or something," Kevin commented. "That's what Uncle Ted told me once."

"Yes, that's the story."

Kevin detected something that flashed across his mother's face. He proceeded. "You know that fall is very cold here in New Hampshire. Along with a flu shot, you might also look into getting a pneumonia shot." He felt he had covered all his bases.

She nodded in agreement as a small dish of cake appeared before her. It was lit with three candles. Her face shone before it.

"Happy birthday, Mom," Kevin said in sing-song. "Make a wish."

She took a deep breath and blew softly. The three candles went out.

"What did you wish for?" Kevin winked.

"That all stories have a happy ending," she replied staring at her birthday dessert.

Kevin would repeat the evening's events to Annie. His mother seemed fit as a fiddle to him.

CHAPTER 29

Open Invitations

October 2014

It wasn't like Meghan not to see her house guests off, but Kevin had assured her after their birthday dinner that it was not necessary for her to be up at such an hour; he planned to depart around four. The only evidence of his early morning departure was the sound of Max as he relocated to the floor next to the bed and began to snore. He grunted and returned to his dreams, feet twitching and nose wiggling — familiar sounds to Meghan.

Four hours later, she sat at the kitchen table, hot ginger lemon tea at her left and pen posed in her right hand. She began to list the many items she needed to attend to on her weekly to-do list. But the pen stayed suspended over the blank page. Meghan's thoughts drifted over the surface of an unusually calm Pawtuckaway Lake. She didn't feel very ambitious this morning. She wanted to go out in her kayak.

The metal recipe box with the newest collection of MacNamara artifacts — postcards and news clippings — still sat on the table before her. The thermometer was already up to fifty-eight, and the forecast promised almost summer-like weather. There had been no sign of Ed Shea's boat.

He had called once, only to inquire about Max, when he had seen Meghan go into the veterinarian's office, and hoped the dog was well.

"We have to get together, soon," he offered.

She hardly had had time to respond when he signed off saying that someone was at his door.

Meghan stood up suddenly; Max jumped to follow. Heading down the hall, she reached inside the closet and pulled out a nylon jacket. Back to her room, she tore off her sweatpants and grabbed a pair of worn shorts.

"Too warm," she told Max.

Back down the hall, she moved like a woman on a mission. She grabbed the cold bottle of water inside the door of the refrigerator.

"So, Max, you are my only spy. Cough it up!" she demanded of the Golden.

If only a dog could speak; he'd been Jack's constant companion for years.

"Probably just as well," she told herself.

She picked up his bowl and filled it with cold water. He tilted his head and then slurped noisily. She headed out the door toward the shore. In minutes, she had untied the neon green kayak and was ankle deep in water, pushing the craft ahead of her. It would be a shame not to skip out on such a day, she thought.

Max barked objections from the shore and then ducked into the underbrush, heading over to find company at the Finches. Their car was visible, parked in the driveway. It wasn't as if he was all alone. She sighed; she was, or so it felt today.

Alice looked up from the window above the sink. Soon, she heard scratching at the porch door. She sighed as she let Max in. Even she had noticed Ed's absence lately. Hinting at the fact had revealed nothing; Bob shrugged and pleaded ignorance. But Alice knew otherwise — something was up.

Hampton Hills was not a large community. People talked. Ed and Meghan had been seen together quite a lot over the summer and early September, but not over the last couple of weeks. Alice watched the solitary kayak head out toward the middle of the lake.

The only real reason Meghan hadn't been a frequent kayaker was that she had just expected Ed to come by. Like a schoolgirl, she was saving her rides hoping he would appear. But he hadn't. And there was no reason she could not go out alone, none at all, she had told herself earlier that morning

Pulling the boat away from the shore line, Meghan carefully stepped inside. Searching for her water bottle, she realized she must have dropped it in her haste. Taking up the two-sided paddle, she began the rhythmic up-and-down motion. The green vessel glided easily on the water surface. The beach and dock quickly drifted behind. Autumn leaves reflected in orange and red on the water before her. A few had fallen, and they danced on the cold surface. The air was crisp. She tucked her hair under her cap and settled her back into the seat. Adjusting the footholds, she focused on the up and down motion, keeping equal pressure on her back, feet, and arms. She was soon in the groove; the boat felt like home. Meghan decided to circle the Island in the Sun. What a perfect morning it was turning out to be. Why hadn't she done this before?

In minutes, she was within a few yards of a small inlet. Her kayak could easily cut through it, since the boat displaced very little water. She would go clockwise and see how her arms felt. She just might head over toward the Dolloff dam, just beyond the island. The burnt orange leaves and brilliant sunshine reminded Meghan of the reason they had begun to call it by the name: Island in the Sun. Today, it appeared almost golden.

Admiring the yellow, she didn't at first notice something else yellow. By the time it was clear that this yellow was not a part of the foliage, it was too late. Just as she came around the northern corner of the island, she caught sight of another kayak. The lemony kayak was exactly like Ed Shea's. Instinctively, she went to raise her paddle in greeting, but stopped.

It was Ed's kayak, but the passenger was not Ed. And it was not anyone she recognized.

Meghan dropped her chin under the visor of her cap to shield her eyes. The woman in Ed's kayak was olive-complexioned with coal-black hair. She was heading directly into Meghan's path. With one sweep of her paddle, Meghan turned the boat. She stopped breathing and felt her shoulders stiffen. Her back was no longer leaning comfortably against the back of the seat. She leaned forward and, as fast as she could, paddled in the opposite direction, careful to make no eye contact with the unknown woman.

Alice had moved herself and Max onto the porch where she had begun to work on an oatmeal-colored woolen scarf. As she picked up her hand to cross over a strand of yarn, she noticed a neon green kayak moving quickly toward the MacNamara dock. The Island in the Sun served as a backdrop, its yellow leaves glowing in the morning sun. Such a short trip, she thought.

But she also caught sight of something else yellow on the opposite side of the land mass: a second kayak.

"How odd," she commented to the air.

She had lost count of her stitches. Dropping her knitting needles, she watched Meghan disembark and move quickly up from the beach and into her camp. There was no friendly wave or even slight glance in her direction. The yellow vessel had headed across the lake, disappearing into the South Channel.

"Enough," Alice announced. "Bob has some explaining to do."

She dropped her unfinished line of knitting and headed down to the shed. Bob had been working all morning. He was busy repairing the skeleton-shaped wooden frame he used to support the boat's winter canvas. He must have gone inside, discarding his tools near a pile of wood shavings.

Without waiting to be acknowledged, Alice barged inside Bob's workshop, blurting out her question. He stood still and waited.

"Okay. What's up with Ed Shea?" she demanded.

"What do you mean?" he replied without looking up.

"I mean . . . where the devil has he been?"

Bob unwound the vice he had been using to hold the sides of his railing apparatus together. He picked up a piece of sandpaper and began to slowly smooth out the ragged edges. He tipped it upright and scrutinized it in the light above. He sent a sideways glance at his wife. He'd been expecting this.

"You know, him and Meghan. He hasn't been anywhere around here in weeks!" Alice's voice was shrill with frustration.

Bob took a deep breath. He bent the railing into an arc the way it would sit on top of his boat. A tarp would be added, and then it all would be secured underneath to withstand the snow and wind of winter. He hoped his friend Ed would show up soon to help him, but he kept this to himself.

"You know something," Alice insisted and poked his arm.

"Look, the guy's busy. He's retired. Let him be," he replied softly.

Bob looked over at his exasperated wife and considered his options.

She studied him. After many years of marriage, she knew that he wasn't one to give out much personal information about anyone. He and Ed went way back. But hadn't it been this very man who knew of Ed's interest in Meghan, and hadn't he encouraged the match? He wouldn't divulge much, but it was worth a try.

Alice sat on top of a nearby wooden milk carton. She leaned against the wall and stared hard. She wanted answers, and if anyone knew anything about Ed, it was Bob.

"You know something," she said again, accusing him. She went further. "Is Ed seeing someone?" Alice waited.

Bob stepped across a pile of woodchips. He reached for a broom and looked into Alice's face.

"He might be," Bob stated flatly.

Alice said nothing. She fiddled with a nail she'd found on the work-table behind her. "Really?"

They both knew that Ed Shea had not dated anyone since Joanne had died. So this news came as a bit of a shock. Who could it be? Everyone knew everyone. Neither spoke.

"Look. It's his business. And Meghan hasn't really given the guy much encouragement, has she?" he added.

Alice's face stiffened. She knew Bob wouldn't be offering up any more. The last comment had a certain defensiveness to it. Clearly, Ed had some reason to put space between himself and Meghan. She knew about the reunion meeting. Who else did? She would not share what Meghan had told her, just in case they were wrong.

"So, is there anything else?" Alice knew to tread lightly.

Bob put down the wooden railing and sat down on another wooden carton. He dropped his shoulders. "All I know is that there is a friend of Ed's sister visiting from California. He invited her to the lake. That's all I know."

"Meghan just met her, I think," Alice offered. She stood up and turned back to look at Bob. "I've never seen a woman hightail it back in so fast in my life," she added with a chuckle. Alice glanced in the direction of the camp next door. "The boats apparently met too," she added pointing toward the island.

Alice needed to think. She really needed to think. One thing was certain: all this was getting no one anywhere fast.

CHAPTER 30

Man Shed

October 2014

"She's my sister. And you are her friend? I haven't visited in a while. You know, my, uh, wife died, not long ago. Well, it's been a few years now."

The woman had said nothing and let Ed go on for what seemed an eternity. She listened politely as if waiting for him to finish his thoughts. She had such deep blue eyes, but her skin was a warm olive.

"I am kind of living on a lake in New Hampshire, and just, finally retired. I took this trip to avoid the people who were at my retirement party. Don't get me wrong — they are very nice people. I said that I was really retiring this time, not just taking a short break and then coming back, which is what I did the last time." Ed paused. He felt out of breath, almost dizzy.

He took a long gulp of the beer he had forgotten he was holding in his left hand. His right hand could still feel the strong grip the woman had left.

"Hi, I'm Lyn Grady," she had said just minutes ago.

Ed looked off as if waiting to be saved. There was no Ted MacNamara here in California. The room was full of laughter and chatting voices. His niece ran past chasing a dog.

He went on. "I've been a principal so long, I wonder what I'll do, you know, with so much free time. I have my hobbies; I build things like birdhouses, for example."

And that was how it began. Lyn Grady told him that she was a retired elementary school teacher. She was half-Irish and half-Italian. She had moved to California after college and decided to stay. But she was born in Massachusetts and planned to vacation there, maybe on the Cape, soon. And was Pawtuck . . . amuk Lake close?

She had been right. It was a muck there right now, his life very murky indeed. Before he knew it, the hours spent with his sister Mary and Lyn proved to lead to a visit. Weren't they all adults? His sister, Mary, was delighted. Of course, she didn't come along. Wasn't she supposed to have come?

This was all Ed had on his mind today. But he finally had time to think about it. Lyn had just left. He had dropped her off at the Manchester-Boston Regional Airport that morning. The days they had spent on the lake had brought back routines and feelings he hadn't realized he missed. As soon as he returned to his empty camp, he had an urgent need to do something, and the shed was first on his agenda. Sitting on the edge of the dock, Ed sipped cold water. The day was warm enough to take a swim, but instead his mind swam.

There was no doubt that Lyn Grady was interested. She had been clear about her feelings in so many ways. Even he picked up on them, he thought. It was he who had reservations, and these reasons ran incessantly in his head.

One day Ed had gone into Hampton Hills to pick up gasoline for the boat. Lyn remained behind chopping vegetables in the kitchen for dinner.

Coming out of the gas station, Ed spotted the familiar dapper shape of Sam Norton. Ed had wanted to bee-line it to his car.

What was Sam doing back? He had split up with Suzy months ago and was said to have moved north. Ed's hand had slipped on the nozzle, gas spilling down his slacks and right shoe.

"Damn it. Why do I care?" he had reprimanded himself.

With only one can filled, he'd driven off without glancing back, hoping Sam had not seen him. He drove to the market and pushed a cart around. Pretending to shop, he filled it with ice cream, chips and soda, things he didn't want or plan to eat. Twenty minutes later, he was back behind the wheel and heading to camp. Lyn was there. What was he doing?

That night Ed turned in early claiming to have the classic excuse: a headache. What he really needed was some space. That seemed impossible under the circumstances.

Lyn was helpful, easy to be around, great company. They took evening cruises on the lake, caught a movie in Manchester and barbequed. He even drove her by Alan Shepard High to show her where he had spent most of his adult life. Truly, the days they had spent on the lake had been very pleasant. As if sensing that he needed some time, she had even taken his kayak out on Pawtuckaway for a solo ride. He had stayed behind to replace a propeller on his motor.

He liked this woman.

But right now, all he wanted was to be left alone. He had projects to do and a life to begin. But the image of Sam Norton blurred his vision. He headed up to the small building hidden under a tall pine tree behind the camp. The metal hut was discolored from years of sap and falling pine needles.

Once he began, he couldn't stop. Today's goal was to empty this utility house; the rusted structure held years of accumulation. The lock hung loosely on a door that hadn't shut properly in decades; it creaked from non-use. The first items within reach were dozens of unfinished birdhouses.

From the cavernous dark bowels of the shed, Ed reached and pulled out pieces of wood, metal and paint pots and made piles like a rock wall behind him. They could all be used to build or finish birdhouses. He had material for roofs, perches, floors, and hook attachments. He could construct the small items for years to come. There were long misplaced tools mixed in, some still in relatively good shape. He was pleased to have discovered them again and placed them apart in a topless birdhouse for safekeeping.

Again and again he pulled, carried, and piled, like a medieval man building a fort. He added bags of unopened birdseed and wrapped two-by-four boards to the growing mound. The musty smell of the paraphernalia filled his nostrils. As the shed emptied, the area in front of it filled. What would he toss? What would have future use? Was some of it beyond repair? Sweat poured from his forehead. He stopped to strip off his soaking wet shirt. He thought he heard a phone ring and, feeling thirsty, headed up to the camp.

Just as Ed stepped into the kitchen, the phone went into answering mode. He filled a glass with ice and poured himself a drink of iced tea. Lyn had made it with fresh lemon. He flopped on the couch and took a long drink. The voice on the phone was feminine.

"Hi. Just getting on the plane. Stopped at BWI. Wanted to let you know I had a great time. Loved your lake," Lyn's voice was deep and warm.

"What do I want?" Ed asked the air.

He glanced over at all the retirement gifts still in the corner of the den. That was his next project. He hadn't even started to send off Thank You notes for them. Finishing his drink and dropping the glass into the sink, he headed back out to the shed.

"One thing at a time," he told himself.

Maybe he could just move into the shed and leave the pile of stuff right where it was. Like a walled fort, he could hide there where no one would find him, at least for a while.

And that thought brought a huge smile to his face.

CHAPTER 31

Old Flames

October 2014

Alice heard an engine before she saw the sleek wooden boat. Where have you been hiding? She thought to herself as she peeked out from behind the bedroom curtains. Ed Shea pulled up to the Finches' dock. She finished making the bed, pulled on a cotton sweater and began to contemplate how to extract some vital personal information from the two men.

Bob was quicker and arrived in time to help Ed tie up the boat. The two men headed up to the camp. Alice was in the kitchen in seconds and began to make orange juice, pulling out a pitcher and two navel oranges. She opened the can of juice already thawed and sitting on the counter.

"Anything cold in there?" Bob inquired as they stood in the kitchen doorway.

"Just me" Alice wanted to reply. "And a Romance on ice." But she restrained herself and instead placed two double-sided plastic glasses on the counter. Slowly, she cracked a fresh tray of ice and plopped cubes into each. Filling the pitcher, she mixed in water, frozen juice and added two squeezed orange quarters, all the time waiting for an opportunity to jump into the conversation.

The men caught up on boat business: when the water would be at its lowest level for the winter, when to work on the docks, when to get their motors winterized. Alice waited, sponging off the counter and pouring herself a glass. She sat opposite the two men at the counter.

"How are you?" she began. "How is retirement so far? We haven't seen you in weeks."

"Good. Good. I've had, ah, some company." Ed poked at the orange peel stuck to the brim of his glass.

Alice sliced another orange and topped off the glasses.

"Would you like some soda water in yours?" she offered.

Ed nodded no. Bob stared hard at his wife, but she ignored the glare.

"So sorry to hear about your friend," Ed said. "How is his wife doing? I missed you both at my retirement party."

"We had to fly out right away. Why do so many things have to happen all at once? She is holding her own. Luckily, she has lots of family around her," Alice responded.

Bob became quiet.

For a moment, they each took a sip of their cold orange juice. Alice slid to the edge of her stool and leaned forward.

"So, Ed, have you seen Meghan? She has a new haircut," Alice inquired brightly.

She didn't look at her husband.

"Ah, no. I haven't. I've been kind of involved with a lot of things. Is she settling in for the fall?" He looked innocently at the woman before him.

"She is. We have a knitting group, you know. There is a group of knitters on the lake who meet regularly; she might join us. She is interested in showing them her old Irish sweater. We think it has the Boyle pattern on it. It was wrapped in cellophane among some of Jack's winter ones in a trunk. Her mother was a Boyle."

This was a good start Alice thought. She had to keep them talking.

"I've been cleaning out the old metal utility shed behind the house. I have so much unused material for building birdhouses. And there are still more boxes long abandoned in the back corner. I can't believe how much stuff that thing can hold."

Bob had gone to the back of the camp and returned with a small rectangular box. "For you. Happy retirement," he announced, and handed the package to Ed.

Ed carefully pulled off the golden ribbon and unwrapped the silver and gold wrappings. "This is beautiful."

It was an accurate miniature model of his Chris-Craft boat. A tiny flag attached to the stern bore the letter "S." Even the cushions on the boat seats matched the forest green of Ed's own vessel. Holding it up with both hands, Ed beamed.

The men nodded approvingly. It was the perfect gift. Bob and Alice knew it.

Alice was ready to guide the conversation elsewhere. "So, do you plan to get back to modeling birdhouses," she went on, "now that you are a man of leisure?"

"Maybe. I sure have enough wood. My daughter has been very successful selling them, too."

"Was she up recently?"

Bob cleared his throat. Alice kept her gaze on Ed.

"No," Ed answered.

There was another pause.

"Oh. I could have sworn that I saw her out in your kayak," Alice continued.

She held her breath.

"That would have been Lyn. She was a guest of mine for a few days, a friend of my sister Mary. She is from California."

Alice finally looked over at Bob with a defiant glare of victory. "I told you so," it said. "Something serious?" Alice was on a roll and she knew it. She couldn't help herself.

Ed stared back at Bob and Alice, dropping his shoulders in a gesture of defeat.

"Who knows," he replied. Then he looked desperately back in Bob's direction.

"Let's take a spin on that new prop," Bob announced, rising from his chair and narrowing his eyes in his wife's direction.

The two men left their glasses on the counter, quickly heading out the camp door and toward the awaiting wooden craft.

"Sorry, Ed," Bob immediately offered. "Really none of our business." Bob untied the boat and pushed them off.

"That's all right. How is Meghan, anyway?" Ed wondered.

"She's okay. Still sorting things out over there." Bob nodded toward the MacNamara camp.

"Sorting. That's it. That's what I'm doing myself," Ed admitted.

Unable to hear the conversation from their seats, Meghan and Alice sat on their separate porches observing the ritual on the deck between the two men. Unaware of the other, the women viewed the scene as the long wooden boat departed.

Once on the lake, Ed played with the throttle. From the shore, you could hear the rise and fall of the motor as it sped up and slowed down. The men onboard Ed's boat listened too.

"Sound good to me. Seems to be running smoothly," Bob commented.

Then without any direction, the men switched places: Bob took Ed's place in the driver's seat and Ed retreated to the back seat to listen to the motor. How many times had these two run this pattern? Like old married couples, it required little more than nodding and thumbs up or down signals to be understood.

But today, Ed seemed to take longer. Bob looked back at his friend, and noticed that he was looking off in the direction of the camp from where they had just left. Bob let the engine idle for a little longer, put it in reverse, and ran it backward for a minute. There was little reaction from Ed. It was quiet as Bob set the throttle into neutral and waited for Ed to take over. Finally, Ed regained his position of captain and Bob sat as second mate. They waited for a few seconds; Bob expected to run the motor at full speed. But Ed didn't move the throttle.

"So, what is the story with Lyn, or Meghan?" Bob finally asked.

Ed shrugged his shoulders and shook his head. He steered the boat up toward the channel, running it at slow speed. "She is very nice. It was a pleasant few days. My sister and she are old acquaintances, so we had much to talk about."

Bob poked Ed in the ribs and winked. "And . . .?" he teased.

"That's just it," Ed blurted out in exasperation. "I just don't know."

The boat had reached the turning point in the channel, and slowly came around Horse Island. Nearby campsites were vacant this time of year. Someone could be seen repainting a sign near the boat ramp area. They looked up and waved as the Chris-Craft passed by.

Looking on the opposite shore, Bob thought he spotted Corky lounging in the sun on the Campbells' porch. If Max had been onboard, their presence would have long been announced. Dogs smelled one another anywhere. Bob wondered when Judy was due. It had to be soon.

They turned toward what locals referred to as the Big Lake. Just before pushing the throttle and speeding up, Ed faced his friend.

"Is Meghan seeing Sam Norton?" he asked.

Bob looked confused. "Why would you think that?"

"I don't know. They seemed quite chummy at the reunion meeting. I was in the building that night to pick up some things, and I saw them alone together," he admitted.

Bob caught a look of pain in Ed's eyes. He didn't know what to say. So that was it. There was more to all of this, after all. He shrugged in ignorance.

Ed put the boat in forward and the motor's sound drowned out any further conversation.

The two men didn't talk further as they headed under the bridge and back toward the camps. They were equally puzzled. It was so simple to determine if an engine and propeller were in sync, but the ways of the heart, well, there was just no owner's manual for that.

CHAPTER 32

On the Opposite Shore

October 2014

Kathleen Shea woke early. Her son Danny had it in his young head that Grandpa Shea had sounded lonely on the phone. He insisted on a surprise visit. The visit was scheduled for the next day. With school closed for teachers' workshop and local elections, it was the perfect Friday plan. By six in the morning, the pair were stopping to pick up fresh donuts and coffee; one needed to be up early to beat Ed. Danny was missing his summer fishing expeditions on the lake. Kate looked over and smiled at the little man sitting beside her in the car.

The diner looked full. The days following Columbus Day weekend marked the arrival of the locals and the departure of much of the summer crowd. She planned to run in and pick out a pastry and coffees to go. Most of the male customers jumping from trucks wore shorts, but fleece vests over flannel shirts revealed that cooler mornings and lower temperatures had set in. In minutes, the two of them would be turning down the road leading to Gramps Shea's place.

Danny had been unusually quiet on the drive up. He focused on the passing colorful trees but said little about the vibrant colors. Katie wondered where his thoughts were.

"You're a tight-lipped fellow this morning," she finally commented. "What's up?"

Danny glanced away again, looking ahead at the dirt road; he seemed distracted by something and was avoiding any direct discussion of it. *Like his father*, Kate thought. She'd need to coax him.

Finally, without looking directly as his mother, Dan toyed with his shirt sleeve and puckered his lips. He looked over at her and crossed his thin arms across his chest.

"Does Grandpa miss Grandma?" he asked.

"Of course. But people come and go in life. It's like a bus ride, really. They say that passengers get on the bus and they get off at their stop. You stay on for your own ride," she tried to explain.

No one's life had been the same after Joanne died. A spark went out in them all. Kate knew this too well.

Danny didn't respond for a minute. Then, as if ready to dive directly in, he turned his head and looked at Kate and blurted out, "Does Grandpa have a new girlfriend?" his voice sounded choked.

This was the real concern. This one was hard to explain to herself. She knew about the visit from Lyn but hadn't said a word about it in front of her son. What had he already figured out?

"I'm not sure, hon. He's been alone for a while. He might like to date someone else." She tried to sound convincing.

"Will Grandpa get married and leave us?" His voice became almost a whisper. "My friend Paul's mother got divorced and married someone else, and they moved away."

Kate was silent for a moment. She needed to address this one carefully. Here was shaky ground. Something caught in her throat. She let her right hand land on her son's left knee and patted it lightly. Moving the car to avoid a rock, she drew in her breath and let it out slowly. She was stalling as she turned the car at a fork in the road.

"Dad loves it here on Pawtuckaway Lake, sport. I doubt that anyone could take him away from here." She was at a loss to say anything more.

They were just minutes from the camp. With all her heart, she hoped that what she had just said was true, at least for now. She needed to say it to herself, and it sounded good to verbalize it to her small companion.

They'd arrived. Dan practically flew from the passenger seat and was inside the camp before Kate could gather up the morning treats. She looked out on the calm surface of Pawtuckaway Lake, and tried to imitate the scene inside herself before heading in. Armed with hot coffee and French twist crullers, she made her way to the camp. Her father would be up and raring to face his day. She felt the camp embrace her in its own warm way. It was so good to be here.

Sure enough, Ed had heard the car motor and stood in his blue flannel bathrobe in front of the kitchen sink. He turned to hear the squeal of his grandson who stood on his tiptoes in the doorway. Ed had not slept well the night before, and the vision of the small figure brought moisture to his blue eyes.

Before Ed could clear the mass of papers and old photographs from the table, Kate had dropped the brown bag of goodies. She headed toward her father, a cup of hot coffee still in his hand.

"Good morning, sunshine," Ed whispered as he placed a kiss on his daughter's cheek.

Dan gave his grandfather a hug and then danced toward the morning treats waiting on the table.

"Guess what we brought? Crullers," he announced quickly.

Kate noticed dark circles under her father's eyes. Dan may have been right; this looked like the face of a sleepless night. Dad had been up for a while. The mass of old pictures scattered over the kitchen table looked like the culprit. What was he doing with all of it?

Kate's eyes widened. Ed began to scoop them up randomly and place them inside the four boxes that lay empty on the chairs. For a moment, Kate saw images of Ed and Joanne in settings ranging from Christmas, to Easter, to birthdays and anniversaries, to various moments from her childhood. Many faces looked back from places and events she didn't recognize. Some remotely resembled people she knew. She helped him clear the table. What had possessed him to bring all this out? No wonder her father appeared disheveled.

"My, look at Mom. Look at you. Still as handsome as ever." She winked at Ed.

"We can look later. I am dying for a cruller. And my grandson needs nourishment," Ed responded.

"School started, Grandpa. I have a new friend. Paul moved away. My new friend sits right beside me. His name is Andrew. I call him Andy. He is from Massachusetts. That's south of here. My teacher is Ms. Lewis. She wears red glasses." Dan had so much to tell Ed as he chirped away like a bird in spring.

The misty morning began to melt away as the sun came up over an autumn-hued lake. The boy was oblivious to the solemnity of the collection in the boxes. This eleven-year-old was at camp, eating doughy sugar and relating all that mattered in a young boy's heart. Ed winked at Kate. Danny didn't notice the silence between the adults.

Danny was right. It was clearly the right thing to have given Ed Shea a surprise visit that morning. The crullers never tasted so good. Dan finished his, and gulped down a full glass of cold milk.

"Can I go down on the beach?" he asked as he got up and headed toward the porch.

They watched him find flat shaped rocks and skim them. Then they cleared the sticky napkins and wiped the surface of the table. Kate lifted one of the boxes and began to pick over the contents, placing sepia-colored photos in a line like a game of Solitaire in front of her. Ed sat down.

"Are you doing some kind of family tree?" she asked. She'd waited until Danny was out of earshot to get into this.

"No. I have been going through the shed in the back and your mother's closets. I never really cleaned out all your mother's stuff. These were packed under a lot of craft materials in her workbench. That box I found up on a shelf in her room. They are all just random. She didn't get around to putting them into albums. She always said that she would. They cover years of our life, and yours. "

"Do you know who all these people are?" Kate used both hands to scoop up a pile and laid more out on the table. "Who is this?" she inquired holding a curling photo up to the light.

Ed peered at the black-and-white image in Kate's awaiting hand.

Dan could be seen tossing a stick from the dock. Ed had no excuse to avoid the subject with little ears far away.

"That was a Fourth of July back maybe around the late 1940s. That is Jack and his dog, Conway. Conway was very old by then and died shortly after. Jack loved that dog."

"How about this one?" Kate proceeded.

"That's your mother and me when we returned from Ireland. That's Sally MacNamara and Jack. Joanne is wearing an Aran sweater."

Jack had a cap jauntily cocked on his head. The sweater looked huge.

"We didn't know what size. They weren't standard sizes over in Ireland, because they were handmade back then. Your mother loved that sweater. Jack wore that cap every Saint Patrick's Day for years. I think Sally had an Irish sweater, too. Everyone brought them back, with a small piece of Irish Belleek china."

Ed looked far off over the lake. His eyes glazed over.

Kathleen was caught up in the stories. She sat down and, picking through the boxes, placed pictures before her father. It was a rare moment, and she became quickly absorbed. Her father had a bit to say for everyone, identifying places, events, and names. He could even estimate the approximate year they had been taken. Very few were marked on the reverse side. Ed's hands trembled a few times, but he seemed comfortable to talk about them.

A picture of Meghan appeared from the pile.

"I met this lady at the craft fair in Hampton Hills. She looks like the lady you kayak with?" Kate noted. "She looks so young."

"Yes. That was taken right in front of Alan Shepard High the year she subbed. That man is her future husband, Tom O'Reilly. They were just engaged. See the snow? It was right after winter break. Meghan was around twenty-two at the time."

The give-and-take continued for another twenty minutes. Kate learned more about the Shea family, MacNamara family and her own parents than she could ever remember hearing. But was it good for her father to dwell in the past so much? Was this keeping him up at night?

Ed selected another collection of old photographs tucked in a faded manila envelope. He poured the contents on the table.

"That man looks familiar. Who is he?" Kate inquired as she pointed to one in the pile.

Ed was silent for a moment. He stared at the face of the man before him. Kate didn't know any of them, but the face seemed familiar.

"That would be Wil MacNamara and Agnes. They are Jack's parents, Meghan's grandparents." Ed took the photo from Kate and placed it down before them. "I wonder who took this one. By the looks of the car in the background, I'm guessing it was around 1928. All was well. They are dressed fashionably. The car in the background shines like a new pair of black patent leather shoes. It was a Model T. Wil was very successful, and Agnes is dressed in her finest in this picture. Look at the mink collar on her coat. Wil was management in the 7-20-4 Cigar factory. This was before it all fell apart: jobs, lives, savings, families . . ." Ed's voice became a whisper.

"What happened to them?" Kate's curiosity was winning out.

"Hard to say exactly. Wil MacNamara left Manchester to find work. Many did."

"It was the stock market crash, right? There was a drought, the Great Depression, and the whole country was affected." Kate could fill in the rest and knew all about it from history books.

"Yes. But Wil MacNamara never recovered. And never returned. Jack became a man overnight. Agnes' life never healed. They were hard times. These pictures show the impact on one family, and I knew them very well."

Ed looked softly into his daughter's green eyes.

She knew it was time to wrap it up. This was uncharacteristic of her dad. He was not one to discuss the past. She had gotten so caught up in the contents of these boxes, it was easy to let the reminiscing continue.

Ed wondered what was worth remembering and what was best forgotten. Jack had avoided what he couldn't change. Some like to understand what was; some would rather not. There was a lot to consider when digging up the past.

Kate and Ed began to collect up the photos just as Dan ran in, holding a frog that he'd found on the beach. Kate and Ed felt relieved as they directed their attention to finding him a large jar.

Ed was considering what to do with the information he had. Reviewing the past with Kate felt like a preview for when he might be expected to do the same someday with Meghan. So many years. So many unknowns.

Ed Shea didn't have the answers yet. But he did know this: the truth has a way of finding its own way, despite every attempt to delay it.

CHAPTER 33

Chasing October

2014

Kevin had done a great job in early summer cleaning up the debris that covered the beach, but the best time to clean was in the fall with the water levels down. The MacNamara beach extended almost twelve feet out by late October, and Meghan knew it was her opportunity to bring the beach down to only sand. Wearing denim overalls, a well-washed flannel shirt and leather work gloves, she headed down into the dry lake bed armed with an iron rake. The heavy layer of leaves awaited her removal.

Maybe it was just her imagination, but it seemed to her that Bob Finch had been especially chatty the day before. The conversation ran through her mind as she worked.

"I have a hole or two in the floor of the shed that needs to be repaired. I noticed it over the summer — Max found it. If I plan to store summer items there, I need to fill them in. Do you know anyone?" she had asked.

"I'll send Pete," Bob had offered.

And as always, true to his word, Pete showed up at eight, sharp, with a truck of mixed lumber pieces, assorted saws, extension cords, tool boxes, and nails. She could hear the buzz of his saw as she stepped off the beach and into the dry lake bed.

"So, how is everything?" Bob had begun. "Any new doings with the upcoming reunion? Have you decided on an appraiser for the place? It really looks nice," Bob had added with a broad smile.

Where to begin, she had thought. No one had confirmed the details of the next reunion meeting. No one had called about the property. And no one — meaning Sam — had called to set up their date. And yes, she had been totally absorbed with the doings of the MacNamara estate: past, present and future. His inquiries felt enormous. She knew he meant no harm.

"Not really," were the words that came out of her mouth. "Everything is fine. Thanks. I need to order some wood for the fireplace."

Bob didn't follow up on any of his initial inquiries.

"Pete gets his wood from this guy in Nottingham. There is some nice seasoned wood there too. I'll ask him about it tomorrow," he had offered.

She raked to the rhythm of Pete's hammer. Her mind wandered forward to the upcoming weeks. There was a Halloween party held at the Hampton Hills Library. Some of the ladies from scrapbooking had asked if she wanted to help. Her thoughts drifted back to the old recipe box again. She seemed to remember a recipe for caramel-coated apples and another for ghost muffins made with marshmallow. The search for holiday traditions had led to the discovery of those old postcards from Wil MacNamara.

Why there? And had it been the work of Agnes to store them in such a hidden spot? Or was it Sally who put them there years later? Meghan had recently felt that Agnes was the most likely suspect. Who wouldn't want to feel close to a family member missing for years? How many of these special dishes were Wil's favorites? How many celebrations was Agnes so painfully aware of his absence? For how many years did she await the next postcard telling her that he was coming home? The discovery of those old messages from the road made the adage "made with love" dig deeply in Meghan's soul. The painted receptacle represented all that went into nourishing a broken family. How long had the receptacle sat under the sink just waiting to be rediscovered, it's secret stored among family recipes?

Stopping to catch her breath, Meghan's eyes surveyed the cool purple surface of Pawtuckaway Lake. She wanted to recreate some of those memories this Thanksgiving. She wanted old-style traditional food, a lit fireplace, and the gathering of the MacNamaras where Jack loved to be most — here.

Max barked and ran off in hot pursuit of a squirrel that had passed too close to him. As if wakened from a dream, Meghan realized that she was thirsty and tired. She decided that a glass of cider would do the trick, so she dropped her rake, slipped off her gloves and headed inside.

A beeping sound announced that someone had left her a voice-mail message. She hit Play and listened:

> "Did you know that there are seventy-two square miles of water up here? The shoreline covers about two hundred miles and the included islands that are scattered all over the lake add another one hundred?
> "This is Sam. I am getting acquainted with Lake Winnipesaukee. Hope to catch up with you. Does next week sound good? How about dinner, Friday?"

"Figures," Meghan said to Max.

The sound of another male voice interrupted her thoughts.

"I need to go into town for some more nails. I might as well take lunch. I'll be back by one thirty. That okay?" Pete yelled from the side porch.

"Yes, Fine. See you then," Meghan hollered back.

She walked to the door and waved. Pete tapped his right index finger on the rim of his hat and headed for his truck. Max and Meghan watched him pull away.

"Max, my boy, we need a plan. Our dance card is filling up fast. There are only two weeks left in October."

Pulling an aqua Pyrex bowl from the refrigerator, half full of tuna salad, lifting a loaf of oatmeal bread and a head of lettuce, Meghan piled up the ingredients for a sandwich. She poured cider into a mug and heated it in the microwave. Then she headed down the hall in the direction of her father's desk. She remembered seeing a yearly planner there. Max followed. Next stop, the computer, to double check emails. She found three.

With one hand on her sandwich, she opened the file of new mail. Anne had left one. It read:

"Wish I had more time. School is off and running. Looking forward to Thanksgiving on the lake.

Anne"

Kevin had also sent one:

"You look like a real New Englander, Mom. Call us about the upcoming family gathering for the holidays. Tommy wants to be dressed like a fisherman for Halloween. Wonder where that came from?

Kevin"

The other two had been left by an email address she didn't recognize: WinRealSN. Then it hit her. It was from Sam Norton up on Winnipesaukee; it read:

"Sorry this week had been madness. Have two huge possible listings on the Lake. Hope you got my messages. Looking forward to dinner.

Sam"

Meghan stared at the three emails. Her social calendar now included grooming for Max, her own haircut, Spooky Nite at the library, baking, phone night for the reunion and dinner with Sam. Each person looked into their future and wanted her there. She felt like she was standing apart and watching them all from a distance. And oddly enough, with each commitment, Meghan kept coming back to the one person she most wanted to talk to —Ed Shea.

CHAPTER 34

Fairy Tales

Halloween 2014

Kate smiled as her son leapt from the passenger seat and headed for the back porch of the Shea camp. She headed in the other direction. Along the side of the shed were rows of finished birdhouses. She counted twelve. Her father had been busy since their last visit only a week before. They were done in multiple colors and stood like a new box of Crayola crayons, all ready for pick-up and delivery. She lifted each tray of four and began to load them into the back seat of her car. The tiny houses were surprisingly lightweight, one of the nice features of his work. It took her only three trips before she headed inside.

"Hi, Dad. You've been busy!" Kate called before entering the camp and placing a kiss on her father's cheek.

Ed stood, his back to her, filling a pot with water. Danny had already disappeared down the hall to change out of his school clothes and store his duffle bag in the back room.

Ed laid two tea bags and a packet of hot chocolate on the counter beside three mugs. He and Kate headed into the front room and took chairs, waiting for the pot to boil.

"Yes, I have. But there are more to do. I tackled the ones that were the most completed and got them done. I hope your friend at the shop in

Wolfeboro still wants them. It is kind of late in the season," Ed sounded a little worried.

"She loved the first four. They were sold in one weekend. Apparently, because you make a wide variety of entrances, customers from all over the country can use them. They're easy to mail too. Liz says that the added details and color combinations draw the eye to them. Some buyers even keep them inside as decorations," Kate assured her dad.

Danny appeared dressed for the camp. Here he could wear old ratty jeans, a well-bleached shirt, and a sweater with tattered sleeves. His school shoes had been kicked under the bed, and summer sneakers dug out from the floor of the closet. The smile on his face was all boy. He dropped on the arm of the chair where Ed sat and stared directly at his grandfather.

"Grandpa, I need your help," he said with a stern face.

Ed looked over at Kate for a sign.

"Oh, yes, Dad. Dan needs to do a library paper," Kate explained.

"I have to go to a real library and not use the Internet. I have to use books, get a librarian to help me and record the names of the books I use."

Dan waited for Ed to collect his thoughts. Ed could barely repress his smile. His grandson seemed relieved to have someone to tell about this huge assignment.

"His teacher is from the old school. She is allowing them to select any topic, but they must visit a library. I think it's a great idea, myself," Kate added.

"I want to look up horses," Dan piped up. "Mom says that there are fairy tale horses here in New Hampshire."

Ed stared at Kate, and then off in the distance. He slowly nodded his head. "Yes, actually, there are. They are called Friesian. I'm sure there would be information about them at the library in Hampton Hills. There are some Friesian horses in Rye, you know. They used to be used by knights in armor. These horses have back legs so strong, they can stand upright. Soldiers could maneuver them easily in battle. They are also very shapely animals with arched backs and feathered feet," Ed began.

"You mean they can fly?" Dan interrupted.

"No. Not that kind of feathering. That means they have a lot of long hair around their hooves," Ed explained.

Kate and her dad tried not to laugh at the image.

"They are handsome horses, and royalty liked them to pull their carriages. They were almost extinct at one time," Ed said sagely.

"Sometimes, you amaze me," Kate shook her head as she spoke. "How do you remember all this stuff?"

The teakettle whistled, and the threesome headed to the kitchen table for hot drinks. Danny's interest was piqued. He wondered if they could go and see the horses.

"Well, maybe. We'll see. But we can start by going to visit Betsy at the library. She works in the research room there."

Danny appeared satisfied. All was well. He plopped four large marshmallows on top of his steaming mug of hot chocolate, and soon his nose had disappeared inside the white fluff.

*   *   *

For Meghan on the other side of the lake, her own use of marshmallows and fluff wasn't going as well. Before her, an open jar of marshmallow fluff was proving to be a sticky problem. She had closely followed the recipe from the box. The chocolate cupcakes had been allowed to cool and were ready for frosting. But so far, the white stuff was stuck everywhere except inside and on top of her baked goods. Rereading the card, she looked hopelessly at the mess in front of her until she noticed something written up the side of the card:

"For best results, keep the spoon heated. Use a cup of hot water and dip the spoon often. The fluff will easily come off onto the cake surface."

This little bit of culinary advice was not written by the same person who had recorded the original list of ingredients. Spiky, forward-slanted handwriting wrote the recipe for the Halloween muffins. But it was the rounded, easy-to-read lettering of Sally's that solved Meghan's sticky problem. She felt as if both women were in the kitchen cooking beside her — a rather spooky image.

The idea was simple: You started with chocolate cupcakes, cut out the top like a cap, and filled the cavity with soft fluff. Then, you added small marshmallows outside, chocolate jimmies for eyes and replaced the chocolate cap. The final treat looked like a ghost was either hiding inside a chocolate can or was jumping out to scare the observer. All in all, Meghan liked the concept and the flavors. She had promised to bring two dozen, and there were still twenty to finish.

Glancing over at the clock on the stove, Meghan noted that she had four hours before meeting Sam for dinner.

The ladies from scrapbooking had not objected when she explained that although she would bake something for the library Spooky Nite, she would be unable to stay and work. The very night she had committed to meet Sam for dinner fell on October 31, and the town celebration too. She was to meet Sam as seven. *Plenty of time for both*, she told herself.

At five-thirty, Meghan filled the sink with sudsy water, and submerged her cupcake tins, mixing bowls, spatulas, spoons, measuring cups and assorted utensils. She would clean them later. She headed in for a shower and shampoo.

Glancing in the mirror above the sink, she was glad she had allotted sufficient time to pull herself together. At both corners of her mouth was evidence of chocolate sampling. Her bangs appeared white with a blob of fluff adhered to the left side. Of course, you never serve anyone anything you haven't sampled. With a bit more frosting, she could be in costume for a Halloween party herself. She jumped into the shower and turned the water on high.

After much deliberation, Meghan had chosen a simple long-sleeve black cotton dress. She planned to add silver and pearls earrings and her silver cuffs. Around her neck her crimson, orange, and gold scarf would add a seasonal touch. In case it got cool later, she would bring her golden-tweed woolen jacket. She figured that she and Sam would drive into Manchester to find a place to eat.

She had dried and styled her hair and was just slipping into her dress when the sound of tinkling came from her cell phone. It sat on the bed. She picked up on the second ring.

"Hey. Hi, I'm afraid that I'm going to be late. There must be some kind of accident on Route 93 South, and I am in standstill traffic," Sam tried to explain.

"Okay." Meghan paused for a second and then thought of her two dozen pastries sitting on the table.

"I had planned to drop off some goodies I made for the Spooky Nite. The scrapbook ladies are helping sponsor it over at the library." Her voice might have sounded annoyed.

Sam paused, and then said, "I have no idea how long this backup will take. I'll get off the next exit and take the back roads if I think that it's not going to break." He tried to sound assuring.

There was a long pause, and no one spoke.

"Look, I'll bring the dessert over. That way it will be there. Why don't we meet at the library?" Meghan suggested.

"That looks like the best plan. I forget how the highways can get on Friday nights. I'll see you there!"

He hung up.

CHAPTER 35

Scary Sights

Betsy Long had been a member of the National Honor Society, attended Saint Paul's Advanced Summer Studies, played in the school band, and proved herself a capable tennis player in high school. She had spent time working in Massachusetts and only recently returned to Hampton Hills to fill in for someone at the town library. Ed had noticed her there on one of his recent visits. She was a college girl now, he remembered.

She looked up and smiled broadly as her former principal approached the information desk. But he was not alone. A young boy, who walked with the same gait, was at his side, wearing an oversized hat of some kind.

"Hello, Mr. Shea," Betsy immediately said.

"Hello, Betsy. Nice to see you again. This is my grandson, Dan. He has a school project to do and needs your expert assistance."

Ed winked uncharacteristically at the young woman. She felt suddenly shy.

Dan extended his small hand and shook it adult-like. He was feeling very smart.

"So, what can I do for you?" She looked toward Ed for direction.

"Well, my grandson is being introduced to some old-fashioned research. He must utilize books and articles to learn about a chosen subject. He is not allowed to go online. We thought that you would be able to guide him in the best direction." Ed nodded knowingly at the woman.

"So, what is your topic?" Betsy asked Dan.

"Horses. Freeshan Horses."

Dan accented the two e's and the *sh* sound.

"Friesian," Betsy repeated, rubbing her chin as if in deep thought. "Follow me."

The two followed Betsy to a room at the far end of the library devoted to local New Hampshire history.

"This would be the best place to start. Did you know that we in our state are important to the saving of this type of horse? They are from Holland. About two centuries ago these animals were almost all gone. At a farm called Runnymede, at the coast, you can see them. This is the same place that the famous horse, Dancer's Image, was from. He won the Kentucky Derby back in 1968. But that is for another report," Betsy said with much enthusiasm.

Ed remembered the woman as a curious student, much involved in high school. She was the perfect one to get Dan excited about this homework. She would make it interesting and keep him from short-cutting, something any boy would try to do.

And as if in character, Betsy looked into Dan's eyes and asked her own question. "May I inquire as to why you are wearing such a hat?"

"I'm dressed up as a fisherman for Halloween. Isn't there a party here later on?" Dan responded with great pride.

"Why yes, there most certainly is. Are you two going?"

"Only after he does his work," Ed answered sternly.

The librarian retrieved three other articles from the stacks for Dan, mostly about the breed and its history. She found another newspaper clipping on the activities of the horse breeding at Rye. Dan was introduced to the one set of hardbound encyclopedias that the town kept updated. Then she returned with a simple book defining the various terms used to explain a horse's anatomy. It was from the children's room, but she didn't tell Dan this. He seemed very much enjoying his serious research in the adult room.

Ed left the boy at a long oak table, immersed in his research, and wandered over to find the latest periodical on fishing. From the next room, he could hear the muffled sounds of hustle and bustle in preparation for the evening event. Through the eight feet high door jamb, ladders had been carried up, and orange and black crepe paper were being hung. A plastic skeleton came next, wheeled in to the corner. It reminded Ed of the one found in the biology department over at Alan Shepard High School. Witches' hats and boots stood on the main desk, along with two ghosts. Candy was being packed into individual bags. He detected the faint smell of popcorn and mulled cider.

As Ed perused an article on making fishing ties, he glanced over at his studious grandson. Surprisingly, the boy appeared totally engrossed in horses. The boy was busily jotting down facts on a blank computer sheet Betsy had provided. The oversized hat had slipped down even further over his forehead, but he seemed unperturbed. Dan had asked to borrow Ed's old and badly worn fishing vest. And with his jeans rolled up, Dan looked more like Tom Sawyer than anything. But Ed was tickled at the choice of costume. He pulled out his cellphone and decided to take a picture while the boy was unaware.

Lining up the frame to capture some of the decorations in the background, Ed carefully aimed his camera eye. He took a breath, held the phone as still as he could and was just about to hit the screen and capture the moment, when someone walked by the doorway. For a second, Ed forgot what he was about to do.

It was a woman in a black dress with a fall-colored scarf draped over one shoulder. And that woman was none other than Meghan O'Reilly.

His first instinct was to get up and follow her. He would be casual, explaining his absence and the visit from Dan. He wanted to assess her reaction and take a measure of the situation. He tried to forget the image of her in Sam Norton's arms the night of the reunion meeting. But his legs moved slowly. He rose from the oak chair and leaned on the table for support.

Before he could get himself around the chair and make his legs cooperate, the same woman walked past the door and out the library entrance.

Maybe it was the increasingly strong smell of melted butter mixed in with the sweet smell of hot cider, but the visceral emotion made Ed feel sick. He sat down and pretended to read. The page was a blur. Dan was totally unaware of his grandfather's predicament.

Minutes may have passed. Ed let his eyes dart back and forth from the magazine and the frame of the door. Then the same black dress passed by again. She was carrying a tray. No doubt it was a dish of goodies for the Halloween event. He got to his feet only to feel his knees buckle — Sam Norton's familiar shape walked by directly behind Meghan.

Were they together? Finally, on his feet, Ed walked slowly over to where Dan was just finishing up his list of book titles. He positioned himself at an angle that offered him a clear view of the entrance to the library, but where he could not be seen. He remembered to breathe.

Time stood still. Dan said something about capitalizing the title of a book. When Ed glanced up, it was just in time to see Meghan and Sam Norton leave the library together.

CHAPTER 36

Old Haunts

During the previous hour, the ladies from scrapbooking had arranged and rearranged the assorted plates on their table of Halloween treats. The eight women kept bumping into one another behind the six-foot-long folding table set up for their display. In keeping with the theme, each had put on assorted costumes complete with make-up and masks, making it impossible to tell them apart. The entire club had contributed to the table, and an intense smell of sugar surrounded them.

In less than two hours, the lobby, main desk, and children's room had been transformed. The custodian agreed to turn off alternating rows of ceiling lights to add an aura of darkness to the library. This added much fierceness to the faces of the glowing jack-o-lanterns scattered on the window sills. Soon, squealing ghouls and goblins would arrive adding an atmosphere of fright and excitement to the evening. Already, it was difficult to tell the real from the imposter. Someone had stood life-size figures of a witch and a glowing skeleton to guard the hallway. There was much to be afraid of on this night. Even Ed Shea wanted to hide.

Meanwhile, Meghan was tossing her jacket into the space behind the front seat of the truck. She had carefully placed the trays of ghost muffins on the passenger seat and on the floor beside her. A quick glance at the clock on the dashboard reminded her that she had plenty of time, if she didn't hit much traffic. Many of the attendees would be walking to the library, but many drove in and the parking was already limited.

She drove into Hampton Hills and directly to the library, spotted a vacant place and headed over. Officer Friendly from the elementary school stood just outside the library lot, taking note of who needed to get in. Meghan pulled up beside him and opened her window. He pointed to the trays. "Those look yummy! You can go right to the ramp. Are you staying?" he asked.

"No. I am just dropping off," Meghan assured him.

"Then just there," he pointed. "There are other spots behind the library for after you drop off your treats."

Meghan pulled up and hopped out of the truck, quickly picked up two trays and headed inside. She was surrounded by hanging cobwebs, grinning pumpkins and costumed volunteers, but it was easy to find the tables of food. She couldn't recognize who was who behind all the masks.

Someone spoken to her. "You can put those here, my pretty," a voice croaked.

Meghan followed the voice and purple fingernails that directed her. The woman had blackened out some front teeth, created a wart on her chin, and added an inch to her nose. Meghan had no idea which of the scrapbooking ladies she was. Carefully, the two trays were set down, and Meghan turned to go back for the rest. "I'll be right back. I have more to get," she had told the witch.

Meghan returned to the truck. She shut off the motor and glanced around to find another place to park. The lot was filling up quickly. She looked up at the church clock across the street; the time was six-fifty. A long line of children had formed on the sidewalk in front of the library. In ten minutes, the event would be in full swing. She was glad she had worn a black dress because already she had evidence of chocolate and fluff on her hands and sleeves.

As she made her way back inside with the remaining two trays, her eyes had fallen on a figure tucked in an alcove under the main stairs. A hand went up to wave. Meghan nodded back. Inside the darkened space sat a woman hidden from view. A crystal ball was perched on a small table, the silhouette of a cat was cast on the wall behind her, and the outline of a bat appeared to fly overhead. The effect was cave-like.

With her arms full and the dim lighting making it hard to see, it took Meghan a second to figure out what she was looking at. Of course, it was a fortune teller for the brave of heart, and it had to be Alice Finch. Meghan had laughed. It seemed the event planners had thought of everything.

Meghan stood before the table. One of the veiled faces took her trays and found a spot for them. She looked down at her own hands and was just about to find the restroom to wash them, when someone tapped her on her right shoulder. She turned. Sam Norton stood inches before her, his face grinning broadly.

"I made it," he had announced. "Just look at all these goodies!" he added.

Meghan had her left index finger in her mouth to clean off a blob of chocolate, and her right hand was sticky with marshmallow, her thumb and forefinger stuck together from the white stuff. Surprised and unable to use either hand, her reaction to being face to face with Sam was to step back. He had tried to lean in and kiss her, but his head was left bent in empty air. He also pulled back and stood staring at her.

"Always in a sticky situation," Sam said eying her hands and the smudge of dark on her chin. His eyes sparkled.

Meghan shrugged looking from one hand to the other and then up at Sam. She smiled and turned back to the table of darkly clad women. "Hope you all have fun," Meghan told them.

"You too," one of the witches replied in a crone's croaking tone.

The room was now full of dozens of costumes. Directions went unheard as children's laughter echoed off the domed ceiling of the main lobby. Sam and Meghan were suddenly surrounded by parents and little masked elves. Small devils, scarecrows, witches, vampires and unidentifiable cartoon characters flitted everywhere.

Sam's arm reached behind Meghan as he guided her toward the illuminated "Exit" sign. She nodded to him, and the two made their way into the growing crowd. They took a left and, passing by the doorway to the research room, the two of them left the library together.

*　*　*

Alice Finch looked over the right shoulder of her first customer. A middle-aged woman had sat down, paid her fee, and giggled as the fortune teller shuffled the cards. Alice placed them upside down on the black velvet tablecloth. Tiny stars seemed to sparkle up from the surface.

"Please pick three," she directed.

The woman slowly selected her cards. Alice swept the others away and stared mysteriously at the spread.

"The first card represents the past. The middle card, the present. And this last card hints at a potential future," Alice said slowly.

The woman nodded.

"Remember, nothing is predestined. It is always your choices that determine what lies ahead."

Alice was speaking to the woman, but her eyes were distracted to the couple she had just seen leaving the library.

There she saw ominous signs, and a shiver ran up her spine.

CHAPTER 37

In the Shadows

October 2014

I t was easy for Bob Finch to make his way toward the library. Youngsters lined the sidewalks outside, all dressed like creatures from another galaxy. He couldn't identify many of the disguises, and wondered how many were based on fictional, computer-generated games. He had to chuckle at some of the faces. Folding the top of the brown bag that contained Alice's lunch, Bob closed the door to his car and glanced up at the full moon overhead.

"Please bring me a sandwich," she had warned him earlier, "otherwise I'll end up eating mostly candy and pastries."

He had to walk a distance. The lot behind the library was full. The street was too, forcing him to park three blocks down near the church. That lot too was filling up fast. He dragged his feet like a kid, making a scratching sound in the dry leaves beneath him. Bob had thought he had plenty of time, but looking up at the illuminated face of the library clock, he realized it was almost six.

He had a clear view of the front entry to the library. The two great red maples that graced the front of the century-old structure were empty of leaves. Their black limbs reached up into the evening sky, adding a kind of bleakness to the Halloween atmosphere. A couple had just begun to descend the steps. Bob instinctively stepped behind the ample trunk of an oak tree. He pretended to answer his cell phone and put it near his ear. The couple was easy to see, and he recognized them immediately.

They crossed the street together. The woman suddenly turned left and headed to the back of the library where a familiar red truck was parked. The man walked a few blocks down a side street and opened the driver's door of a sporty white car. She drove the truck around from behind the library to meet the awaiting white car. Both cars drove past Bob who remained hidden in the shadows of the tree.

Bob's heart beat fast. He shook his head at his own strange reaction. Flipping his phone closed, he walked out from the shadows and raced up the steep steps of the library. He had to catch his breath before pulling the ancient oak doors open and stepping inside.

He found Alice just as she was completing a reading for a young girl. She looked up. Bob would always get a kick out of his wife's "Fortune Teller" look, but this outfit took the cake. She toned it down for casual readings, avoiding any appearance of black magic. The effect of tonight's get-up made her really look like something out of a circus act.

"Maybe you'd have preferred a wart of newt or an eye of toad for dinner," he couldn't resist blurting out. "It's ham and cheese. I added a pickle."

"I have something to tell you," she said. "We have a pickle."

"I know." Bob nodded

Alice began to open her lunch bag. There was a pause in business as the speaker announced that apple bobbing and Pin the Tail on the Devil were about to begin. Alice looked up at the same instant as Bob did. He nudged Alice's left arm — Ed and his grandson Dan had appeared in the doorway to the research room. Danny headed in the direction of a contest; Bob waved in Ed's direction. In unison, Bob and Alice took a deep breath.

"Too late," Alice said aloud.

"Yeh," Bob added.

Bob Finch had known Ed for many years. They had had many good times together. Ed and Joanne were one of those couples: no one could image them not together. But Bob also knew that Meghan held a special place in Ed's heart.

Bob stood stiffly beside Alice, neither knowing what to do or say. Clearly, Ed had seen the couple leaving the building.

"Meghan was here and left with Sam Norton," Alice whispered to Bob.

"I know," Bob replied. "Did Ed see them?" Bob needed to know.

"I don't know," Alice said slowly.

Danny had moved over to the donut swing and was being blind-folded. Ed Shea was nowhere to be seen.

* * *

Olive Smith had begun her career at the Hampton Hills Public Library as a volunteer when only a teenager. She had no degree in library science, but she knew the contents of every shelf in the building. She loved the old *stacks* where clippings and newspaper articles had been stored for decades. She made local news her business. Ed Shea was responsible for Olive getting a full-time job there. She had what we would now call a learning disability and was socially quite shy, but her mind could file away information better than any noncomputer he had ever come across.

She didn't get involved with such celebrations as the one going on downstairs that evening. She didn't object; she just watched and did her job. Walking along the balcony above the main hall, Olive spotted her former principal and waved. He was up the stairs, glad to avoid any conversation with the Finches' at that moment.

Taking two steps at a time, Ed was soon chatting with Olive. Their heads leaned in together and side by side, they headed to the New

Hampshire room. Olive loved to be of help, and helping Mr. Shea was top on her list.

"Mr. Shea, I have those articles you asked me about. I made you copies of some, so you can take them with you." She handed Ed a large manila folder.

He held it firmly in both hands. "I've been organizing family records. It is quite a complicated project. This could help me place dates on many of the documents. I'm tracing my family back to Ireland. It's been quite fascinating, but there are so many gaps," he explained to the woman before him.

"I also put the other information you said you were curious about in there," Olive added innocently.

"Thanks, Olive."

Olive blushed with pride. She waited for Ed to add some further explanation for the unusual request she had filled, but he was not forthcoming. She smiled. "I hope this helps."

Ed looked off down the hall as if an answer lay there. Young voices echoed up through the library ceiling and filled the silence as costumed winners took their awards in the rooms below. Clapping ensued.

"Thanks again," Ed called back to Olive.

He headed down the hall and back to where he had left his grandson below. He hugged the folders close where they lay, tucked safely inside his zipped jacket.

CHAPTER 38

The Date

Halloween 2014

It was midnight. Meghan wrapped herself tighter inside the woolen blanket. The chair felt cold beneath her. She looked overhead at the dark sky of this unusual Halloween night. She was glad she had some old rag wool socks on her feet and Dad's woolen cap on her head. What a sight she must make. But she needed to be beside the water of the lake to think. The water rushed softly to the shore.

Her date with Sam Norton had been appropriately set on this night. If ghosts from the past were supposed to be close at hand on this hallowed eve, hers certainly were. Tonight, she had visited the halls of Alan Shepard High School without even setting foot inside. Did her own spirit wander the halls? Sometimes, she had to wonder.

Max leaned against her chair and groaned. He had showed up when she pulled into the camp driveway. He came from somewhere next door. Bob had kept an eye on him, offering to leave the door open while he dropped by at the Spooky Nite with Alice's dinner. The evenings were getting colder on the lake, and Max needed a place to go when everyone left. She would have to be aware of his whereabouts now as November approached.

The entire date with Sam passed before Meghan. She laid her hand on Max's head.

"All those goodies make me want chocolate," Sam had remarked as they left the library earlier that night. Then he asked, "Do you have some comfortable shoes with you?"

That was the first hint that the evening was going to be a bit more casual than she had planned.

She had followed Sam's car away from the lines of cars still arriving at the library. He had turned west toward Manchester. She turned on the truck's heater to warm her cold bare legs.

Luckily, she had a pair of sneakers on the floor beside her. Why did the evening require comfortable shoes? The car with the plate "ISELL" passed another car. She did the same. Twenty minutes down the road, Sam took a right off the highway and onto Exit 9 South. He pulled into the parking lot of the Puritan Restaurant and parked out front. Meghan pulled into a vacant spot across the lot. Sam got out of his car and headed over.

She rolled down the window; he leaned in.

"Wait here," he instructed.

The outside ice cream window was closed for the season, so Meghan watched as Sam disappeared inside. He'd picked up a large brown bag and was back beside the red truck in minutes.

"Do you have those shoes?" he inquired.

Meghan pointed to the floor on the passenger side.

"Perfect. Put them on," Sam said as he headed back to his own car.

All thoughts of a romantic evening began to fade in Meghan's mind. She slipped her heeled shoes off and put on the worn peds found rolled up inside her sneakers. As she tied the laces, she watched Sam open his trunk and take out an assortment of items: blankets, bags, and jackets.

Just go with the flow, she had told herself.

As Meghan pondered over the evening's events, somewhere, a fish came to the surface. A splash was heard. Maybe it was a pinecone falling.

Max jumped and growled. Meghan readjusted her seat and wrapped her blanket tighter around her shoulders. The events of the evening continued to unfold in her head.

She'd stepped from the truck wearing her sneakers and woolen jacket. The air had felt cold. As if in response, Sam handed her a pouch.

"There is a nice down jacket inside this. Just pull it out and put it on. Here is a hat too," he'd instructed.

Soon, the two of them crossed the Daniel Webster Highway, leaving their cars. Down a dark road they'd walked in silence, heading for Dorr's Pond.

As they neared the water, Sam began. "Did you know that Dorr's Pond is named after a realtor?"

"I did not," Meghan responded.

"Back in the 1800s, a George Horace Dorr bought the property. It was called Ray Brook before that. The famous local Revolutionary War hero, General John Stark, had owned it earlier. There had been a saw mill here," Sam continued.

Sitting on the edge of Pawtuckaway, Meghan realized that the voice she had been hearing was the one she had listened to for years. It was Mr. Norton, the teacher, giving a lecture. She had to smile.

Warm inside his down jacket, Meghan found herself amused by the change of plans. These were his plans, his invitation, his way. What else did he have in mind?

Sam proceeded to open a portable blanket and spread it on a grassy area few feet back from the pond. He unzipped the sides and invited her to sit. He also wrapped her legs in a second blanket, and then turned his attention to a large brown steaming bag.

Within minutes, Sam had carefully placed two paper plates on the ground and sorted out a whopping plate of chicken tenders, two Greek salads, pita bread and French-fried potatoes. From his backpack, he presented two individual bottles of white wine. From the pockets of his own jacket, he removed two plastic wine glasses and some white paper napkins.

He had brought them dinner.

"Are you warm enough?" he inquired.

Meghan had had little to say. "Oh, yes. I'm plenty warm."

As they ate, the pond whispered its presence. Soft waves brushed the shore, just as Pawtuckaway did hours later as she reflected on the evening's events. Sam's voice could be heard long after he'd fed her French fries and poured her wine.

She felt transported back in time. He was in teacher mode, just the way she would always remember him. She felt more like an audience. But the old Sam was back there, and so was she.

"Dorr's Pond was used to harvest ice back in the 1860s," Sam had said as he waved a French fry toward the water, using it as a pointer.

Meghan remembered collecting samples from the water of Dorr's Pond to bring back to the biology lab. There the students would grow one-celled animals. In her class, she'd created a blueprint for them to follow so that they could write up their lab reports.

From his backpack, Sam then took out two white cups full of ice cream. He had maple walnut, and of course, hers was mocha chip. With her mouth full, she had had little to say. She chose to let the evening unfold. Or maybe, she just didn't want to spoil the moment.

"Where did the time go?" Sam asked in a soft voice. "We were so young."

Meghan picked at her ice cream and watched Sam's face take on expressions of sadness and joy. He stopped talking. It was her turn.

She began to mention the names of the students they had shared. She wondered what became of them.

They remembered the female student who had fallen into Dorr's Pond on one of their class trips and had required Sam to wade in and carry her out.

"She had lost a contact lens," Meghan recalled. "Her name was Jacqueline. We dubbed her Jacqueline the Queen after that."

They laughed at the memory. Sam looked at Meghan as if to say more, but he seemed to have decided against it. Instead, he went back to the pond history.

"Elephants from traveling circuses had been brought here to be washed and cooled off. You won't see that ever again. Most circuses are totally out of business now."

The moon rose behind the pond and it was as if there were two bodies of water: one real and the other its reflection. Sam tossed a rock, and the smooth surface rippled into small circular rings that expanded to the shoreline.

Max adjusted himself and Meghan was brought back from her spell. She looked over at the Finches' place and saw the light in the bathroom flick on and off. They were both back from the Spooky Nite. Max settled down beside her as if to tell her that he was staying the night.

Sam and Meghan had sat on the side of Dorr's Pond for almost three hours. They had talked about their time teaching together, the many personalities of their shared pupils, about their marriages and about where they were now.

The night air was getting cold and they noticed through the trees that the parking lot at the Puritan was almost empty. So the two of them packed up their Halloween picnic and began walking down the dark road back to Maple Street, when Sam suddenly took Meghan's hand.

Together, they put all the items back inside the trunk of Sam's car. Then he had walked Meghan to her red truck. Leaning in, he had held her in his arms and kissed her long and deeply.

Pulling away, Sam held her face in both his hands and sighed. "I'll give you a call," he had said in a hoarse whisper.

Then they had driven their own vehicles to their own homes, alone.

Meghan rose from her lakeside seat, and Max got up to follow. She closed the door to the camp, padded down the hall and climbed into bed. In minutes she was asleep, still wearing Sam Norton's down jacket.

CHAPTER 39

Duty Calls

November 2014

S ometimes, when Kate Shea was sitting on the camp couch reading, her face angled just right, the evening sun caught her profile and the sight took Ed's breath away. She looked exactly like her mother Joanne. He would hold the moment as if his wife was there in her usual spot. This retirement had its limits. Some days Ed felt free and useful. Other days he had to remind himself that the past was over and that nothing could bring it back. The upcoming holidays would be a challenge with all the memories they held.

The shrill sound of his whistling teapot pulled Ed back to the present. He made himself a fresh cup. As he poured milk in, his thoughts turned to the contents of the manila folders Olive had given him. He had procrastinated while his grandson was visiting, but they awaited his review. He wondered what else he would learn about the past from them. He intended to begin with the topic of Wil MacNamara. Although after recent events, he doubted that he and Meghan would be discussing the information. The scene of her leaving the library only a week before flashed before him. Olive had mentioned that Jack MacNamara had asked for similar information years before and at the time had added more data to the collection.

"Jack MacNamara came in once asking about the so-called incident on the train rails. He wondered if other newspapers had reported it the same way. He wondered about witnesses and a timeline, just like you have," Olive had explained.

Ed had purposely said nothing.

"The body of Wil MacNamara was found along the Merrimac River. This was reported differently. One article claimed it appeared to be a suicide. But one newspaper didn't come to that conclusion. At the time, there were a lot of hobos riding the rails. Details about men disappearing for months, years at time, were not unusual. Families often never knew what became of many."

Olive was very businesslike when she related this to Ed. He admired her discreteness. She didn't ask him why he wanted to know this. He wondered himself.

"There are initials on some of these files. I can't make them out. It looks like a third person was also curious about this death, "Olive had added.

The excuse Ed had used to begin this library research was his investigation into his own Irish heritage. All the photos and dilapidated albums he had unearthed left him with many odd images of faces he did not recognize, and the ones he did were often mixed with faces from the MacNamara family. How far back did the Shea and MacNamara families go? Did they live in close proximity even in the Old Country? He had in his folders records of births and deaths as well as marriages. Where would he start? He took a sip of his tea just as his phone buzzed.

"Hi. Is this Ed Shea?" a pleasant female voice asked.

"Yes. Who is this?"

"It's Jay from the school. How are you?"

"I'm well. What can I do for you?"

Jay was the most recent addition to the Alan Shepard library. She had begun working the previous year. In fact, Ed had hired her for computer skills. She had proven to be good with the students and quick to direct them with all of their technical and traditional needs.

"I realize that this is very short notice, but you were the first person I thought of to call," Jay went on to explain.

Ed closed the folder he was about to open, and listened. What could he possibly be of use to as a retired principal? The new administrator seemed quite capable, and he'd promised himself that he would not be drawn back or get into any kind of administrative difficulties. He was not the principal anymore and respected the position of the new hire.

"We have our usual Veterans Day assembly coming up. Our guest speaker has bailed. I wondered if you could come in and do the honors. The theme is leadership," her voice became soft.

"I'm not an expert," Ed responded. "This assembly is on what day?"

"It's actually being held on Monday morning. We have a half day on Friday and Veterans Day falls on Tuesday . . . so school is closed."

Ed could hear Jay take a deep breath on the other end of the line.

No one said a thing for a few seconds.

"I know it is a lot to ask on such short notice and all. I just felt that you would do a great job. At least you know where the teens are coming from. So many speakers really can't identify with this age audience."

Jay was very convincing.

The deal had been clinched. Jay had caught Ed when he needed to visit his school. He knew he could do this. He wanted to.

Closing the unread folder, Ed hung up the phone. He had a speech to give and little time to prepare.

CHAPTER 40

November Plans

The new image on the wall calendar depicted the scene of Thanksgiving preparations. A Pyrex bowl in deep brick sat full of bread stuffing. Next to it were half-peeled potatoes and what appeared to be a pitcher of milk. Dough sat rising in a nearby pan. A perfectly browned turkey appeared in the backdrop. Meghan could almost smell the feast.

Her own holiday plans had just begun. Halloween had only been a week ago. She had only received emails from Sam since then.

It appeared that Sam Norton was taking Winnipesaukee Lake by storm. He had at least three potential listings on the lake. One was in Alton Bay. His new office address was in Wolfeboro, but by the sound of his messages, he was traveling to all parts of the area.

"There is a small window of opportunity between now and the end of the year," he had emailed late the previous night. She had read it the following morning.

"No one wants to move over the holidays, and once the snow arrives, well, you may as well wait until spring," he had written in a later entry.

Meghan understood that he was new in that area and that this was his job. Still, with all the feelings she had and the holidays coming, she felt out of touch with him. His plans to be in southern New Hampshire didn't seem to be very soon, although he did suggest that it would be. Soon was a relative term. And November for her was the start of a busy season, one in which she wanted him to be a part.

Looking at the calendar, she began to circle dates. The two biggest occasions were Thanksgiving and the reunion. Both required some planning and commitment on her part. The best thing she could do was to begin with her own plans and just let the *Sam thing* be.

Louise, Ed's former secretary, had also emailed Meghan. She informed Meghan that she had prepared an incomplete list of members of the class of 1974. She had many with emails as well. Louise had wanted to remind the reunion committee that they had a meeting to finalize many of the details of their event. Caterers, decorations, advertising all needed to be confirmed. They had a get-together there at Alan Shepard for Friday, November 7, and Louise wondered if Meghan would be attending.

Pawtuckaway Lake appeared barren. The water had been lowered and the MacNamara beach stretched about twenty feet longer than normal. The dock looked like a giraffe abandoned in a desert with its long legs and awkward footing. Wind and rain had washed away what was left of the colorful foliage. Winter pulled at Meghan. She shivered. Was it the seasonal change or her own mood that created such a cold, grey scene?

She moved toward the computer. Quickly, she replied to Louise's message. She would come by Friday and help with the reunion committee. Louise almost immediately asked what she might like for lunch. Apparently, the parents of Alan Shepard students were donating a bag lunch for all the reunion members. Meghan selected tuna fish and an apple.

Her next thought was to contact her family. Picking up the phone she dialed Anne first.

"Hi, sweetheart. I know that you are at work, but I'm calling to remind you about Thanksgiving. I still want to hold it here on the lake. Call me and we can talk about the menu."

Ted was next.

"Hi, dear. It's Mom. I know you are asleep, but I thought I'd better contact you so that you can plan. We will hold the family Thanksgiving dinner here on Pawtuckaway. Let's figure out who could bring what. We will have to delegate. Call me when you can."

Satisfied with her own proactive actions, Meghan pulled out a blank computer sheet and began a list of what she would need to do a dinner here. She had never done such a complicated meal in such small quarters. Her real cooking equipment was stored in the cabinets back in Arizona. This would truly be like camping out. This oven was barely big enough to fit a large chicken.

She began to write: holiday napkins, matching tablecloth, candles . . . She wanted to have nuts and dip with chips; she'd make deviled eggs. The dinner would have to depend on what side dishes or vegetables they all liked. She would need potatoes, carrots, tiny onions, and peas. She could skip the peas, but Tom liked them. Gravy — maybe Judy could make that.

The list grew. She was accustomed to the luxury of a second refrigerator as well. So many things she used were in another house thousands of miles away. If she needed extra space, she would just have to place some items on the porch — the weather was cool enough. The food would be safe as long as Max didn't find it!

She added the spices she would need for her stuffing and penciled in celery and cranberries. Her cell phone went off.

"Hi, Meghan. This is Roberta, from scrapbooking. How are you?" a cheery voice asked.

Quickly, Meghan tried to match up a face with the name. She could only picture the costumed and disguised images of the ladies at the recent Halloween party.

"Hi. I'm fine."

"How is your family album coming? We haven't seen you in a while."

"Good. I really enjoyed your summer meeting. I hope to have more pictures from the upcoming holidays. What's up?"

"Well, the reason I'm calling is to ask if you were planning to come to the annual Pie Walk. It's like a cookie walk but with pies. We sponsor the event along with other clubs. It takes place on Thanksgiving evening in the basement of the Town Hall. We raise money for the Shriners."

Meghan turned her list over. Her mind went into overdrive. Wouldn't this be fun for her family? Such a neat idea.

"You only have to bring one pie. We generally get six slices from each. We charge three dollars. Ice cream is extra. We get quite a turnout."

The woman made it sound so easy. How could she refuse?

"I could bring an apple pie," Meghan found herself saying.

"That would be great. It is our most popular flavor. Just drop it off any time on Thanksgiving. We have a key, and the place will be open all day. Thanks so much! Look forward to seeing you and your family there!" Roberta hung up.

Thanksgiving was certainly unfolding. The idea of adding something new to their family traditions pleased her. It was good to get out and do something after eating. Everyone didn't have to go, but those who declined would miss out on the pie.

Meghan began to circle more dates on her November calendar. She took another sheet of paper and made a note to herself to put warmer blankets on the beds. She would need to dig out the other quilts her father had stored. Also, she needed to purchase some soda and beer, and maybe champagne. If she put it all down, she wouldn't forget.

This was better. She felt just the act of moving forward had put her in a more festive mood.

Her mother Sally had a great apple pie recipe. Meghan would need cinnamon, nutmeg, and Granny Smith apples. They were supposed to be one of the best kind of apples for baking. Or was it Cortland? She would double check that.

Her thoughts went back to the spices she needed for turkey stuffing. The familiar image of a box of Bell's Seasoning flashed among the myriad of possible necessities for a proper holiday feast. The seasoning already contained sage, rosemary, and thyme, she thought. There was a small patch of rosemary left in her mother's garden. She could gather more from there.

"All I need is cinnamon, sage and some thyme," she said out loud and heard herself chuckle. "At the moment, I am neither wise nor do I have the time to worry about it. So I'll just use cinnamon."

This was something Jack MacNamara had said and always laughed at his own play on words.

Meghan headed for the old recipe box stored back under the kitchen sink. The holiday season had begun!

CHAPTER 41

Veterans Day 2014

The folders Olive had given Ed sat on his kitchen table. He had other thoughts now. The folders held no answers to what he would say at the upcoming Veterans Day assembly. Instead, he headed for his bedroom, pulled on rag wool socks, a red thermal undershirt, a flannel shirt, and a pair of corduroy slacks. Quickly, he grabbed his barn jacket and brown leather gloves. His black wool cap hung on a hook beside the porch door. He grabbed it as he headed out. Ed needed to go for a walk.

Many camps along the road stood vacant this time of year. The rest reflected only darkened windows; their residents were probably at work. It was mid-week. Ed pictured his own office space at Alan Shepard High School. Someone else sat behind that desk now. But they needed him, and he would return to deliver a speech.

There was a spring in his step as he headed up the steep dirt road that ran behind his camp. He thought about how a dog would have been nice company for such a day. That idea was for future consideration.

What did he want to tell the students? How many Veterans Day speeches had he heard given in that auditorium through the years? So many didn't leave much of a message for the young audience. What might he say to them about leadership?

He was quite a history buff himself. His shelves were full of biographies and history tomes. He had taught history briefly before being promoted to principal. He often wished he had stayed a bit longer in the classroom, but the opportunity presented itself and he accepted. Who were the historic figures most Americans admired? And why?

Ed vaguely remembered Dwight D. Eisenhower as president. Eisenhower had been a general before being elected. He knew war and so wanted to maintain peace.

JFK represented youthfulness. He inspired young people to serve. The sixties were an era of change, with civil rights demonstrations and adventures to the moon. Despite JFK's own personal weaknesses, he was a leader who left his mark on history.

Richard Nixon brought shame to the office of the president. Watergate felt dirty. Nixon felt he had to cheat to get reelected. He didn't have faith in the voters to choose, even though they had chosen him twice.

These students would remember both Bush administrations. Why did we vote in two members of the same family? The senior Bush had an outstanding military record. First lady, Barbara Bush, was remembered as a symbol for the cause of literacy in America. Mother and wife of a president, she too represented feminine leadership of her time.

With Obama, we could proudly add a black president to our list of leaders. And although racism was not eliminated in America, the rise of Obama reflected an enormous historic landmark in a new direction.

Ronald Reagan was our oldest president to date. He rode horses like in the old westerns. He once told someone who tried to turn off his microphone at a political event, "I paid for this mike." That event had been held right here in New Hampshire. Reagan demanded that the wall dividing Berlin should be torn down. Even Soviet leader, Mikhail Gorbachev admired his American counterpart. Did his words impact the eventual act? Both of these men were leaders who changed the world.

Why do some aspire to greatness while others choose to follow? History books were full of those who stood up and took charge, some in office, some on the battlefield.

Ed had reached the part of the road that led to the boat launch. He could walk out almost twenty feet into the lake on dry ground. From this vantage point, he could make out the golden color of the state beach. The park was closed for the season; the beach sat empty. To his right the outline of Dolloff Dam appeared black. The entire scene felt stark and grey under the pale November sky.

When had these leaders felt the responsibility to act? What were their motives? His own parents were often referred to as the Greatest Generation. What was it that united them?

FDR had led a country from a wheelchair. He carried America through both an economic disaster and a world war.

Weren't Hitler and Stalin leaders? Why did entire countries follow them?

Winston Churchill rose to greatness when England and the world needed him. Ed had a mishmash of images in his head. Where was the common thread?

He headed back up the boat ramp toward the return road to his camp. Vietnam and Korea had been the wars of his generation. For this graduating class, it was ISIS and Afghanistan. These represented yet another kind of fanaticism. Was our American way of life being threatened? Who would be our next president in the upcoming 2106 election? What kind of leader would we choose?

Leaders surfaced when they were needed. Some were unlikely candidates. His Veterans Day speech would remind the upcoming graduates why this country was worth fighting for. He wanted to plant a seed of pride in them.

He wasn't just their old, retired principal Mr. Shea.

CHAPTER 42

Empty Halls

Without intending to, Meghan had pulled her red truck into the same spot she had first parked in back in the spring. The lot was equally empty. Louise had mentioned that school was on a half-day schedule that Friday, which was why the reunion committee had access to so much of the school. She noticed a truck parked at the front. It was from a local pizza/sub shop. No doubt her tuna sub was among the lunches being delivered. Meghan felt excited about being at Alan Shepard. She wondered who would be there. Sam's name had been among the ones contacted on the original email list Louise had sent her.

The halls were free of students. A few lights had been left on in classrooms. Meghan's heels echoed on the wooden floor as she passed the glass windows surrounding the main office. Louise spotted her and waved her down the hall toward the cafeteria. She was on the phone, but Meghan got the message. Apparently, lunch came first, and Meghan was hungry.

The image of Sam and her stumbling around in the dark flashed before her. She directed her eyes down the corridor leading to the reunion volunteers.

Passing by the auditorium on her way to the cafeteria, Meghan heard a male voice. If she didn't know better, she would have sworn it sounded just like Ed Shea's. From the gist of Louise's email, Meghan thought that all the teachers' workshops were being held over at the elementary school. The doors to the big hall were open slightly, held ajar by a rubber stopper. She stopped and listened. It sure sounded like Ed. Her curiosity got the best of her, so Meghan opened the door slowly and slipped into the darkened hall.

A high wall extended along the back of the auditorium, separating the rows of numbered velvet seats from the entrance. It was easy to stand there and not be seen. She remembered this from her days teaching there. You were able to keep an eye on disruptive students and interfere before things got out of hand. The only visible light today was focused on the stage. The remaining areas were shrouded in darkness. Meghan leaned against the back wall and slowed her breathing. There stood Ed Shea.

Ed was apparently practicing a presentation. No one else was around. She decided to listen.

> "It is great to be here to speak to all of you today, not as your principal, but as an American.
>
> I know many of you. But in less than three years, you will all have either graduated or gone on to jobs. And possibly, families of your own.
>
> I have been in attendance for many speeches given in recognition of our veterans. I hope my message for you is different."

Ed paused to take a sip of water.

> "Veterans Day is for the living. It is held to recognize those men and women who served their country and returned. Yes, we remember all who died, but today is for those fortunate enough to have come home safely, those who returned to begin a life here."

Ed stopped to turn his paper and clear his throat.

> "In your lifetime, you will observe many acts of courage and cowardice. Many of you will serve in the military. Many will know friends or spouses who do. You will come in contact with veterans casually and in formal

settings like this one. They all have something to teach you. They all have their stories, and have earned the right to tell them.

I could lecture you today about the many faces of heroism that fill our history books. I am sure you would recognize most. When you are older the list will include people that you voted into office. Presidents can lead us to war, or toward peace.

Always vote.

My father referred to this day as Armistice Day. It was also called Remembrance Day, for it was on this day that formal hostilities ended with Germany in 1918.

Even I wasn't alive then."

Meghan muffled a giggle. Ed paused.

"We Americans like our long weekends. So, in 1968, with the signing of the Uniform Holiday Bill, this day was incorporated into a weekend. It took until 1975 for President Ford to return it to its original day.

Would you like your birthday changed to another day just for the convenience of your family?"

Ed stopped again. Meghan didn't move.

"World War I ended formal hostilities on the eleventh hour, of the eleventh day, of the eleventh month of the year. November 11 is the true Veterans Day.

And so, it is with great honor that I speak to you today about this holiday. I hope wherever you are and whatever you decide to do on Tuesday, you stop to remember those who served, suffered and survived.

They came home."

Meghan wanted to clap. She waited until Ed walked offstage and had shut off the stage light. She headed straight for the ladies' room to wipe the tears from her eyes — such a great speech.

She hurried down to the cafeteria where most of the reunion committee had already finished their bag lunches. Quickly, she glanced around. No sign of Sam. That old familiar pit came into her stomach. She doubted it was the tuna fish sub before her, but she couldn't seem to bring herself to eat.

Meghan was back at Alan Shepard High School, with Ed Shea's voice echoing down the empty halls.

CHAPTER 43

Unclear Signs

November 2014

Max hadn't slept well over at the Finches' on that cold November night. The poor canine had been let out at both houses, wandering between the MacNamara porch and the neighbors' deck. Did he need a visit to the vet? Did he have a urinary tract infection or some such thing? Or was it that the dog too felt restless on that dark night?

Alice had already been up twice, hearing Max scratching at the screen door. The time between visits made her assume that Meghan was at her own porch door doing the same thing. The dog flopped wearily on the warm wool blanket Bob had left on the kitchen floor. Wooden floors were rather cold this time of year. Max sought a cozy bed.

Bob had been asleep. Being a deep sleeper, he seldom woke up for much. But on this fall night, his wife was up and Max was doing rounds; he heard them both. His wife had not been sleeping well lately and he knew why.

Halloween night had been over a week ago, but both Bob and Alice had seen Meghan leaving the scene with Sam Norton. Ed Shea had not been by their camp since. His absence spoke volumes. Ed had to have seen the couple together.

What could anyone say? Bob knew Ed had feelings for Meghan. Bob was also aware that Meghan wasn't over Sam. The return of the real estate agent upset everyone. But Ed Shea would not intrude or judge; he was too much of a gentleman to say much.

What was Alice doing? Bob was aware that she had been doing more of her "gypsy stuff," as he affectionately referred to her card readings. Had Alice been doing someone else's spread? No doubt it was Meghan's, he had decided.

Pretending to need to use the bathroom, Bob had wandered into the half-lit kitchen. Alice sat at the counter, the Rune cards spread out before her. What did she see? He never took any of it seriously. Neither did she really. But the Rune cards had been a part of her life, and he didn't question them. After all, her aunt and Irish grandmother had used them as well. They were merely an aspect of her own cultural upbringing. But lately she had referred to them with more frequency.

He paused at the threshold. She was so deep in thought, he had to clear his throat to get her attention.

"When are you coming to bed?" he asked softly.

"Oh, shortly," she answered slowly, as if speaking from somewhere else.

He waited. She offered no more. Max rose and circled the woolen bed pulling his golden body into a tight shrimp-like circle. Moaning, he settled down again. Bob continued back down the dark hall.

Alice stared at the five-card spread before her. She let her own racing thoughts pass, and fixed her mind on the situation at hand. She had done three separate readings on Meghan, and each one had a similar message. Three identical cards appeared each time. She had shuffled thoroughly. The repeating cards were Disruption, Standstill and Journey.

The first card represented great change, a liberation even. Events beyond anyone's control were at hand. It was as if someone had been asleep and was awakening, finally seeing things clearly. The question was, who?

Was Meghan realizing that she had always been in love with Sam? Or was the greater reality that Ed Shea had a history of being in the shadows, but like a firm hand he remained a solid force in Meghan's life?

This card represented a ripping apart of what had been, as plans seemed to fall apart. The concept of radical discontinuity shook Alice as it reappeared in the reading. Would Meghan follow Sam and break away from her ties here on Pawtuckaway Lake? Was the spell Sam had on Meghan still strong since that year they'd spent at Alan Shepard High together?

Again and again, the second card, Standstill, revealed itself. It warned that the existing situation was an entanglement that was frozen. One could only wait for a natural thaw. Spring was a long time in the future. It was only November. Could this love triangle survive the holidays? This card worried Alice the most. Was there no movement forward?

The last card was the Journey card. For the life of her, it was the most confusing. This message spoke of a long and steep trip. How far would Meghan go to be with Sam? Alice sighed. Would the camp be sold as Meghan moved a hundred miles north and took the longer road to be with him? This one was selfish thought. Alice wished her neighbor happiness. Why did the possibility of Meghan leaving Pawtuckaway Lake bother her? It was up to Meghan.

"Silly woman," Alice admonished herself. "They are only cards."

The Runes were not for her to manipulate. She had been instructed never to try. They only offered the reader insight into their own heart. Alice had too much emotion invested. It was not like her.

She looked over at the sleeping dog. Standing up, she glanced over at the MacNamara camp. All lights were out. Sipping the last of her cold tea, she gathered the cards and stored them in the leather pouch.

"Max," she whispered, "why are you here tonight? Is Meghan at sixes and sevens over there?"

Alice knew that Meghan had visited Alan Shepard High on official business that afternoon. The reunion committee meeting had been held there. Had Sam come too?

She tucked her Runes into the kitchen drawer. They were only signs. They were not intended to be used to judge, predict or impact. Just because she and Bob wanted Meghan and Ed together didn't make it right for them, any of them. It was just that the warm days of summer were slipping by and the coldness of November seemed to have stalled the happy arrangement. She closed the kitchen drawer with a shove.

"Let it be," she whispered.

She had pastries to bake, knitting to complete and social obligations to attend to over the next few weeks. The message of the cards was what it was. But why did they feel so disquieting?

CHAPTER 44

Holiday Anticipation

November 2014

"I really liked your speech," a male voice shouted to Ed Shea as Ed dropped groceries into the trunk of his green jeep. It was Scottie Price, a senior at Alan Shepard.

"Thanks, Scottie," Ed called back.

"We miss you," a distinctly female voice yelled. It was Scottie's girlfriend. Ed didn't know her name.

He had to admit it— it had been nice to be a guest at his old job, if only for the morning. He had continued to receive emails from staff and students complimenting him on his performance. And it was even nicer not to be the principal. This was a noticeable difference for Ed.

All in all, adjusting to retirement had its good days and bad days. This morning, he was loading up on extra food and looking forward to his visit from Kate and Danny. The unexpected email from his sister Mary however left him, once again, uncertain. She wanted to come east with her friend Lyn Grady to do some Christmas shopping. They planned to go north and shop at the closest LL Bean Outlet. They looked forward to experiencing winter weather before it really was winter. Was the Thanksgiving break a good time to come, she had wondered.

He had mentioned the Pie Walk on the eve of Thanksgiving and the official lighting of the town tree in Hampton Hills Common. He must have created an image that sounded so picturesque to those in warm, sunny California, and had unintentionally set himself up for the visit. This ran counter to his own worries about all that was unfolding in his New Hampshire world. He'd made it all sound too good.

Early September had felt so easy. Despite the opening of school without him, Ed had spent some days kayaking with Meghan. They had gotten into the habit of spending leisurely hours together. Hadn't they planned to plant an herb garden, and to begin some potting inside over the winter months?

When the mornings became cool, the two had gone out for coffee. Everyone in town had seen them together. The trip out to visit California was overdue. Lyn Grady's visit hadn't been serious for him. He liked what he had with Meghan. Now he wondered what it had been.

How many times had he shuffled and reshuffled the folders containing data on his Irish ancestry? He had planned to share much of it with Meghan. She had also led him to believe that the MacNamara project she was working on overlapped with his. It only made sense to coordinate their separate work. He had found much helpful material from Olive in the town library stacks. Now it all lay collecting dust on his desk. Things had changed since Halloween.

Some days he wanted to burn the folders. Some days he wanted to drop them off when he knew Meghan would be out. Some days he picked up the phone to invite Meghan out for a simple coffee, but he froze. And some days he felt like old, retired principal, Ed Shea. Who wouldn't choose the flashy Sam Norton over him?

Ed had made himself scarce since that night at the Halloween party. Alice and Bob Finch had called and left messages checking in on him. He owed them a call back. Olive had emailed him that the extra information he had checked out was due back. He feigned a head cold and had spent a lot of time raking leaves into a collection of thirty oversized brown bags. His yard never looked so clean.

He had made it a point to make copies of the library documents on his home printer. There were records of births, deaths and marriage certificates. He had unearthed additional information worth sharing with the MacNamaras. But lately he felt in no rush. Ted had not given him permission to share what he had with Meghan, and he felt no obligation to present his findings at this time.

So, Ed headed his vehicle out of town, his passenger seat overflowing with groceries. Passing the library on his right, he noticed that the only remnant left of the Halloween Spooky Nite were two gigantic orange pumpkins perched on the top steps. Glancing at the giant oak doors, the image of Meghan and Sam flashed vividly before him. Something red caught his eye. Was it a red truck parked in the lot behind the structure? He looked back at the road, and drove on.

He focused on Route 101 E. He was off to Pawtuckaway. Mountain Road felt somewhat deserted this time of year. Even the Mountain Road Trading Post seemed to have gone into hibernation. Colorful maple leaves blanketed the ground, while green pine trees leaned into the building as if to protect it from a snowy future. Winter was just around the corner. The white shrink-wrapped boats sat as reminders of the white stuff to come.

Ed was proud of his recent speech. He was proud of the birdhouses he was selling. Kate had more orders for him to fill. He felt that company in for Thanksgiving would be good for him. Danny could be relied upon to entertain. Kate would help with making Joanne's recipe for pecan pie. He wondered if Meghan's grandson Tommy would be up. He'd deal with that if it happened. No need to worry any more than needed.

His mind wandered back to the red truck behind the library. It probably wasn't Meghan. Anyway, he wasn't of a mind to see her, yet.

CHAPTER 45

Missing Archives

November 2014

Olive Smith could feel her cheeks redden. She wasn't good at fibs, but she was bound by rules at the library. Among them was confidentiality. She could not disclose who it was that had taken out the requested material. She could only say that the item was out and that she would let the next person know when it had been returned.

"I expect that material might be in the lower archives. I would need more time to locate it for you," she stated firmly to the woman before her.

"It might be helpful to me. You see, I am putting together a family history. I have a surplus of photos, but little to go on concerning chronology. I figured that being a small library, you would have files on many of the residents. Even newspaper articles would be helpful, I think," Meghan explained.

"Yes. A lot of people want to know their family histories. In this town, many of the stories overlap and sometimes the story of one person leads to more about other local families. I will call you when the requested information is returned," Olive lied. She bit her lip to stop from saying more. She knew the collection was with Ed Shea and felt that this woman might even know him. But rules were rules.

"There's no rush. I was just in the area and, with the upcoming holidays and all, decided to come in and look into it. My goal is to have most of my album finished by Christmas. I'd like to present it in album form to my family by then." Meghan smiled at the bashful woman before her.

As long as she was there, Meghan decided to head for the periodical section. She perused some magazines with colorful Thanksgiving covers. Inside, she looked for a few recipes to add to her growing menu. She found a simple one for cranberry relish. She noted that one woman added chives to her mashed potatoes for a mild oniony flavor. This year, a new tradition was being made: Thanksgiving on the lake. She would use the recipe cards in Sally's box and add some things of her own. Satisfied, she headed for the oak doors.

The memory of leaving with Sam only weeks before forced her to pause before reaching for the brass doorknob. She danced down the front steps and headed for her red truck. She had been lucky to find a spot just behind the library. The idea of inviting Sam to join her and her family for the holidays popped up again. And again, she felt that it was too soon. They were still only casual. Why make hasty assumptions? Joining them all at the Pie Walk would be less awkward and would say less. She pulled the door to the truck behind her and sat for a second. A green jeep drove by the road in front of the library. Ed had such a jeep. He used it in the winter on the dirt roads around the lake. But she figured that it probably wasn't him.

Instead, she let her eyes fall on the list that sat next to her. She still needed some holiday-themed napkins, plates and glasses. She had the spices required for most of her recipes. Her list reminded her to stock up on soda. Should she buy the fruits she wanted for her cornucopia? Some of the items could wait.

Annie had left Meghan another email. She apparently would not be staying the entire holiday weekend. She and the new teacher had plans to go to Boston. Meghan smiled at the thought of Annie in a new relationship. Holidays often did that to people.

She pulled the red truck into the drug store. Her nose had been dry, and she needed some nasal spray. The shelves held marked-down Thanksgiving décor. Already, on the ends of the aisles, stood Santa Claus and reindeer. Candy canes and ornaments piled up in boxes, ready for the next onslaught.

"One holiday at a time," Meghan mused.

"I know." the sales clerk agreed.

Bottles of wine and champagne filled the wall. Meghan needed some extra alcohol on hand. She would visit one of the state liquor stores later in the week. Kevin had said that he would also be bringing some. A rack of miniatures reminded her of the picnic date she had at Dorr's Pond: Sam's individual servings. She picked up one bottle and smiled to herself.

As Meghan waited in line to pay for her purchases, another image came to mind. The night before, after sorting the old recipe cards and flicking through the postcards from Wil MacNamara, she had fallen asleep on the couch. She had a dream. In it, Tom was alive, and they were back in Connecticut. Annie and Kevin were small. It was a former Thanksgiving when Tom would carve up the bird, and the children would make dibs for the drumsticks. Tom liked to mix the meat on the platter, claiming that despite all modern claims, both dark and white meat were healthy. Dark meat was much moister and didn't require gravy. He had finally settled the dispute and given both Annie and Kevin their own drumstick. The scene was warm, familiar and so real. She had awakened disoriented.

The colorful painted recipe box came to mind as Meghan loaded her truck. The postcards revealed another man on the road looking for a job. He was tired and homesick, but optimistic. The way the homecooked meals sat on cards alongside the postcards seemed to will Wil MacNamara home. How difficult were holidays for a family wondering where their father was? The tone of the messages scribbled on those cards said to Meghan that Jack never stopped believing that he would return to Manchester and the home-cooked meals that awaited that day. Why hadn't he returned?

A white pickup pulled in front of Meghan. Her mind had wandered off again. A screech of brakes brought her back to the present. She veered, and the truck passed her with a horn blast.

Mountain Road came into sight, looking quiet this November day. She continued up the hill. Max would be waiting for her.

From this perspective, the Thanksgiving ahead promised to be a fine family affair. The entire MacNamara tribe would be together on the lake. It would be a special holiday to remember.

Meghan could hear her mother Sally's voice say: "It will all work itself out."

And no one was looking forward to it more than Meghan.

CHAPTER 46

Message Delivered

November 2014

Max jumped up from his nap and barked. Meghan hadn't heard anything, engrossed as she was in a pile of photos she had labeled: "The 1930s." The familiar recipe box lay open on her father's desk, the yellowed recipe cards stacked together like a pack of playing cards. The weathered postcards sat apart, ordered chronologically according to the days Wil MacNamara had sent them. The pairing of recipes and postcards would forever be imprinted in Meghan's memories long after her collection of family memorabilia was completed.

From the front of the camp came the familiar sound of three taps on the door. She heard Alice Finch.

"Hello. Just me," Alice hollered.

Meghan stood up and headed for the kitchen. Max led the way. When she arrived, Alice was crouched down giving Max a good side rub. He moaned with pleasure.

"Hello. Come in. I was just about to put on water for tea. Want some?"

"Perfect."

Alice nodded and took a seat at the kitchen table. Max curled up at her feet.

"Haven't seen much of you. Looks like you're preparing for some holiday guests," Alice began, pointing to the cornucopia on the table next to Thanksgiving-themed napkins. Then she ran her hand over the woven tapestry of the tablecloth, decorated with leaves in shades of brown, gold and amber. "This looks so nice." She smiled up at Meghan, remembering how plain the place had looked only a year ago when Jack MacNamara lived there alone.

"Thank you. Yes, it is coming up so fast. I'm mixing china and paper. Without a dishwasher, it is easier if I use both. I can relax with it being just family. Are you having company in?"

"So far, it is Bob and me, plus a cousin of his and maybe a few friends from the lake. It isn't firmed up, yet," Alice admitted.

Meghan pulled down a large pumpkin-walnut bread from the top of the refrigerator and began to slice it on a plate. From inside, she found a container of soft cream cheese. While Alice chatted about her possible dinner guests, Meghan set two cups on the table, and headed back to the stove. The pot soon began to steam and whistle. Alice chatted about the upcoming Pie Walk in town and how she had finally decided to bring a Boston Cream pie.

Meghan noticed circles under Alice's eyes and mentally noted that she seemed tired. She hoped all was well. Holidays always demanded so much, and so many people picked up colds. She hadn't seen her neighbor except for a few friendly waves since the Halloween night at the library. She wondered if Bob had had any recent contact with Ed Shea. Both women had left his name out of their conversation so far, intentionally.

"I'm making apple pie for the walk. I think the Pie Walk is such a neat idea. It brings the community together and gives those alone someone to share the day with," Meghan commented.

"So how many do you think you'll have here at the camp?"

"I plan on Annie, but she won't be staying. She has a new beau and will join him later. Kevin and Julie will be here with the kids. She intends to bring a pie since we will be a big group. I think she said something about making strawberry-peach. So, I plan on six. This table will handle that many."

Meghan sat and sipped her tea.

Alice's hands felt for the cards she had tucked inside her jacket. Her visit had an agenda. It was the spreads that were keeping her up at night. They were only cards, and she knew well enough to never put too much weight into them, but these repeating themes seemed to want to be heard. She was here to relay that.

The two chatted about past holiday disasters: lumpy gravy, burnt turkeys, dry stuffing and runny pie filling. Meghan thought of the recipe cards in Sally's handwriting.

"Apparently, my mother had a secret to guaranteeing moist stuffing," Meghan offered. "She always added chopped apples and celery, and did not stuff the turkey. Her stuffing was served as a separate dish."

They sipped their tea and nibbled on the bread. For a moment, both were silent.

"This bread is so good with cream cheese." Alice chuckled as she wiped some cheese from the corners of her mouth.

Finally, Alice put her cup down and Meghan rose to refill her tea. Alice reached inside her pocket and tapped the pack of Rune cards.

"So, I have to ask," Alice paused, "have you and Sam gotten together?"

Meghan stood before the stove, her back to Alice. Her hand gripped the handle of the kettle. Inside the thick kitchen glove, she could feel moisture forming behind each knuckle. Slowly, she refilled Alice's cup with a teabag and poured hot water into it. She turned and carried two steaming cups to the table; her eyes never left her own hands.

Alice bit her lips and waited.

"Bob and I saw you leaving the Halloween event together."

Meghan offered Alice some honey for her tea. She refused. Meghan sat down.

Alice stirred her tea and smiled as Meghan stared off without saying a word.

"I'm sorry to be so inquisitive, but I need to tell you something."

Meghan still said nothing.

"Well, I have done some Rune card spreads on you. And I have to admit that there is a pattern . . . one that I can't really deny or fully understand. The signs are a bit, well, dark."

"Dark. Like in unclear, hard to tell, or ominous?" Meghan wondered.

"Actually, they see rocky roads ahead."

"What were the cards exactly?"

Meghan leaned forward. Alice pulled the Runes from her pocket and placed the three troublesome cards on the table. They were: Standstill, Disruptive, and Journey.

"These cards appeared in all three spreads. I shuffled carefully and there were days between readings. They indicate a lot of rockiness. They also imply a very steep climb. But there is an underlying hint of a stalemate. These aren't as difficult to apply. But the Journey card . . . This one isn't usually found among the other two. It is a contradictory message. Are you going away?" Alice added in a weak voice.

Meghan's face gave away nothing. She stared at the three cards and back at Alice. It was her turn to answer. "Yes. Sam and I did have a date. Yes, there has been a lot of correspondence between us, although mostly online."

Alice put both her hands on the table as if to demonstrate that she was literally showing all of her cards. She couldn't leave without saying all that had been bothering her.

"Now, it's your turn. It's about Ed Shea."

Alice waited for a response.

An eternity passed.

"He has become a stranger. Bob finally just showed up carrying a jar of my cranberry relish. It was used just as an excuse to drop by."

Meghan made a face.

"It's as if you and Ed are taking separate paths. He seems to be avoiding you. I do know that he has been sorting through a lot of old stuff since his retirement. There are school-related items, some of Joanne's things and apparently family documents and photos. Bob got the impression that Ed had some revelation about the MacNamara family that he thinks you might be interested in. I would guess that he feels uncomfortable just coming by or leaving it with you." Alice sat back in her chair and let her shoulders drop. She felt a burden lift. "Does this make any sense to you?" she asked.

Meghan's mind raced. Still there were so many unanswered questions in her MacNamara story. What did Ed know? Was is important to her own research? Was she wasting time trying to fill in all the gaps? Did it matter?

"I have a lot more to find out about if this research is to be complete. I wanted to present all of it to my family by Christmas. I wondered what Ed has that I don't already know. I do know that the Shea and MacNamara families go way back. They may have known one another even in Ireland! I am sorry that he feels so awkward."

Meghan offered Alice more bread. The two finished their tea, and the conversation turned to how the days were getting shorter and the nights were getting colder. They joked about wearing gloves and having cold feet. There was more on both of their minds, but no real way to say it. So much was still up in the air.

Alice had delivered her messages. Only Meghan could decide what direction she would take or how it all applied to her situation.

The two women cleared the table together and gave one another a hug. Max followed Alice to the door and, to Meghan's surprise, followed her home, leaving Meghan alone with her own conflicting thoughts.

CHAPTER 47

Cold Weather Forecasts

November 22, 2014

Bob Finch sat in his Adirondack chair. Max was quick to spot him and to park his reddish-brown body beside him. Bob wore rag wool socks, leather boots and a fleece-lined barn jacket. Over sleep-flattened hair, he had donned his winter cap. Thermal lined gloves protected his hands on this crisp morning. Winter teased the corners of the day; storm-weather outerwear was gradually being donned to fend off the colder temperatures. At five in the morning, only the steam rising from his hot coffee held any warmth in it. Pawtuckaway Lake sat still and grey before him. No one else was probably sitting out on such a chilly morning, he mused.

Alice's predictions were often accurate. Ed Shea's remoteness was a clear sign of his avoidance of the lady next door. The most recent developments between Meghan and Sam Norton only reinforced the facts. Ed had recently admitted that he was, indeed, having guests in from California for the Thanksgiving break. Bob's mind was unsettled that morning. But what could he do?

Glancing at his full suet feeder, he felt the coming cold. Winter birds had begun to show up in large numbers; he listened and watched as blue jays, woodpeckers, juncos and chickadees chirped and pecked at his suet block. It was November 22, only five days until Thanksgiving. The morning sky looked threatening and dismal overhead. Shivering, he took a big swig of his coffee.

His friend Ed was going down a path Bob didn't like. Jack MacNamara's daughter was as well. What was Bob missing? Adults could be so confusing. You couldn't tell them what to do. He just wished that he could.

Clearly, the ladies liked Sam Norton. Ed Shea had said as much to him the day Bob delivered a jar of Alice's relish. And there was more. But what was it? There was this unclear area between Meghan and Ed. No one could venture in there. Someone seemed to be withholding facts. But what was it about? This was what was bugging Bob: he liked facts.

Bob stood, and he and Max walked out on the exposed bottom of the lake. When the lake dropped over the winter, another world opened. The dog sniffed dried remains of sticks, grasses and leaves. Overhead, Canada geese honked noisily by. Across the lake a few lights twinkled in the darkened windows where residents were getting up to face a new day.

You didn't need contact with a fortune teller to sense events taking their own course. The holidays often had a hard impact on people. No one wanted to be alone then. How many engagements occurred this time of year? Ed missed Joanne. Bob missed Ed. Imagine if Alice was gone? Bob sighed.

The summer months had seemed idyllic. Ed was spending time with Meghan. Sam Norton was engaged to Suzie. All the kids had hit it off. It all felt like ages ago now. Bob wondered if any of the children would be up for the holidays. Halloween had been a turning point.

From his vantage point out on the lake, Bob could make out Ed Shea's dock. He could see white reflected on the shrink-wrapped boat. He and Ed used to go to the marina together with their boats, helping one another trailer them and park them for the impending snow and ice. This year, Ed had done it without Bob. Yes, things were complicated this year.

The porch light flicked on and off on the Finches' porch. A hand waved. Alice was up. She had been sleeping better since she had her little talk with Meghan. Across the lake, a small break in the sky revealed a rising sun. But the clouds were tenacious. The sun would not win. The horizon remained dark and overcast.

He waved back and called Max to follow. They headed to the natural shoreline of the lake. Usually, Thanksgiving was his favorite holiday. It was less chaotic and commercial than Christmas. He loved turkey and gravy and extra ice cream on hot pie. He had lived long enough to realize that life changes, and every holiday is different from the last. Even so, Bob just liked some things to stay the way they were.

If Ed Shea needed more than the company of Dan and Kate and him, then so be it. If Meghan's heart melted every time she encountered Sam, what could he do? He spotted a perfect flat rock, and skimmed it across the dark, smooth face of the lake. It ricocheted six times before sinking into the water's depth.

He and Max turned to face the lit camp. A warm kitchen awaited them.

One small act can alter a life, like the stone he'd just thrown, and can reverberate in unexpected ways.

He had to let things go and allow life to decide the path it took. His coffee was cold, like the raw nip in the November air.

CHAPTER 48

Stormy Weather

November 23, 2014

Meghan curled up and pulled the Sunday newspaper closer to her. It was only four in the afternoon, but the light outside was fading. She turned on the lamp beside her and found her reading glasses.

From the porch, Max's familiar bark warned her that he wanted to come back inside. She rose and opened the porch door. He clearly wasn't going to remain outside on this grey afternoon. Glancing over at the Finches, she could see smoke rising from their chimney. The sky was full of clouds.

Max had recently declared the braided rug near the couch his spot. After a quick trip to his water bowl, he did a complete circle to get his entire body into a warm twist. Then he groaned and settled down. Meghan retrieved her newspaper.

She turned on the television. Sunday was a perfect time to catch up on what was going on in the world, and to spend some quiet time inside. She slipped out the many market flyers to see what was on sale this week. She would make one more trip to buy fresh vegetables, bread and fruit for her centerpiece.

"Look, Max, there is a sale on grapes."

It was October 23. The family would be coming in for Thanksgiving. By Wednesday, her guests would have arrived. She had two days to clean up, prepare and make up some beds. She felt excited and very grateful.

Sam had texted her that he would be down for the Pie Walk. This too was the best way. She and Sam were just starting to see one another. It seemed too premature to invite him to Thanksgiving dinner. She had a full house, and she would be busy with them.

Even from her seat, she could see that the sky over the lake looked unusually thick with clouds. She flicked the remote to find out about the local weather for the next few days. The meteorologist was pointing and explaining that they were tracing some kind of storm coming up the eastern coast. Temperatures were predicted to be quite cold here in the northeast and more weather seemed to be moving in from southern Canada. Radar followed the path of low pressure near the mid-Atlantic, but the combination of two storms might prove to have an impact on New England. We could expect precipitation, but it was all too early to know how much or when.

Just as Meghan's lips formed the word "snow," her cell phone rang. She jumped up to get it and managed to climb over Max and grab it before it went into answer mode. It was probably Annie. Meghan half-expected her daughter to bring her new interest to some part of the family celebration. She might have to set another place at the MacNamara Thanksgiving table, and that was fine with her.

"Hello," Meghan said, and listened for a familiar voice.

"Hi. Mrs. O'Reilly?" a deep, male voice replied.

"Yes. This is Meghan O'Reilly."

"It's Larry, Larry Bureau. I'm staying at your home in Arizona. I'm you tenant," he explained.

It took a second for Meghan to switch gears and realize who this male caller was.

"Of course. Hello, Larry. I haven't really spoken to you in a while. Is everything all right?" she asked.

This was the first time neither Kevin nor Ted was the one giving her updates on her property. It seemed odd to be talking directly to her tenant.

"Well. I am sorry to call, but everything has changed here. I didn't think that you knew."

"Knew what?"

The young man cleared his throat. "Mrs. O'Reilly, I did my best to clean up. But you know that I am in the Reserves. I was called in to go to Afghanistan in May, and the governor, as you know, requested assistance on October 22."

It was all swarming inside her head.

"The damage here in September, you know, the flooding and severe storms? We are in one of the worst counties hit in Arizona. On November 5, President Obama declared us a disaster area. We will get some federal help, but I will not be able to be here."

The voice settled down on the other end of the phone. Meghan breathed.

"Mrs. O'Reilly. Someone needs to be here."

"Larry, I had no idea it was so bad. My sons told me about some property damage, but that was when you were there. I understand."

Meghan didn't know what else to say.

"Mam. We did our best to repair the damage. The winds did a number on your roof, and the rain washed out much of the back foundation. I leave tomorrow."

"Thank you, Larry. I will get in contact with my brother and my son. I need to get there immediately."

"Sorry. I knew I needed to let you know."

Larry was off the phone, leaving Meghan far away from pie walks and family arrivals. All she knew was that a storm was converging on New Hampshire in the next few days. She needed to fly to Arizona before the biggest travel day of the year arrived. Someone needed to be there, and she knew it had to be her.

CHAPTER 49

Unexpected Turnout

Week of Thanksgiving 2014

Meghan had never been so happy that she had Internet connected to the camp than she was that night. She immediately went online and booked the next available flight from Manchester to Phoenix. She also notified her neighbors there when she would arrive in Arizona.

Next, she emailed Ted in England about the situation and, before he could object, told him she would handle it. The last email was to her son and daughter. Annie could come up to the lake; there was plenty of food. As it turned out, Annie decided to remain at home, and enjoyed a cozy dinner with her new beau.

Tommy developed a bad sore throat and was sent home from school on Tuesday, November 24. It turned out to be the flu, so Kevin, Julie and Beth celebrated their holiday at home. Only Beth was inconsolable. She so wanted to see a wild turkey. She was sure there were many on Pawtuckaway Lake. Tommy was allowed extra ice cream for medicinal reasons, and to make up for missing the Pie Walk he had heard so much about.

On November 26, New Hampshire would encounter one of the worst snow storms in its recorded history. Wet, heavy snow would down power lines, roads would close and roofs would collapse. Airports, schools and businesses shut down as well. It would go on record as the fourth greatest power outage experienced in Granite State's history, with over two hundred thousand people without electricity for days. Many eastern states were paralyzed.

Meghan had been correct. The skies over Pawtuckaway Lake were ready to act. Bob had felt the oncoming storm as he sat at the edge of the lake brooding over something he did not want to happen, and Alice Finch and her restless nights somehow knew from her Runes that there was danger lurking ahead.

Sam Norton could not travel the snow-packed roads down to the celebrations in Hampton Hills. He spent the holiday in Wolfeboro.

Few folks in New Hampshire enjoyed hot turkey with all the trimmings on that Thanksgiving in 2014.

The small town of Hampton Hills in New Hampshire might have been in the dark and without hot gravy and turkey, but attendance at the Pie Walk was an all-time high. Word got around quickly that the town basement was full of pie, whipped cream and ice cream. It was soon full of flashlights, lanterns and headlamps. Most of the attendees bundled up and, putting on warm boots, walked to the event with pies in tow. Perhaps the slices were a bit slimmer, but no one complained.

Ed Shea came with his daughter Kate and her son Dan. Ed's sister and her friend from California were unable to fly in to New Hampshire because of the inclement weather. All flights into Manchester were cancelled.

Meanwhile, Meghan arrived in Arizona in temperatures well into the sixties. There was extensive damage to her home. Her neighbors had already begun the process of repairs and were more than happy to get her caught up. She celebrated Thanksgiving with them and was grateful that the damage she expected was not nearly as bad as it could have been.

Alice Finch and Bob arrived at the Pie Walk. It was obvious that Meghan was absent, but no one asked them directly about it and so they just enjoyed their desserts. They noticed that Sam Norton was missing as well.

A brief note left in the Finches' mailbox read:

> "Dear Bob and Alice,
>
> I had to fly to Arizona to deal with severe storm damage. I sent Max over. Please care for him until I can return. I will be in touch. I hope to be back in two weeks.
>
> Extra dog food in the back shed.
>
> Thanks for Everything.
>
> Meghan"

*   *   *

Ed Shea stood at the door of the town office surveying all the commotion in the half-lit basement hall. He could barely make out faces under the headlamps. The place felt warm from all those who had come. The air smelled sweet from the pastries. He stayed until everyone had left, and helped clean up. He never saw Meghan. He never saw Sam either. His friend Bob winked at him conspiratorially. He never had chance to ask what it meant.

Ed didn't know Meghan's whereabouts that Thanksgiving night. He would find out later, but on that cold snowy night in New Hampshire, his only wish was that wherever she was, it was some place warm and safe.

And he missed her.

CHAPTER 50

Standstill, Disruption, Journey

November 28, 2014

E d Shea sent the Finches a quick email before putting on his snow-shoes. He needed no map to find his way along the shoreline and unplowed roads around Pawtuckaway Lake. Bob had indicated at the Pie Walk that he had something to tell him and wouldn't tell unless Ed heard it all in person, and Ed sorely needed a physical workout to get up the courage to talk. The Finches were some of his oldest and dearest friends. He needed to see them. The trip over took him longer than usual, but he took his time eating trail mix and sipping water along the way. The roads were deep with snow, but the trees presented picturesque scenes along the route, so laden with the thick white blanket of new snow.

Max was the first to notice the sight of Ed's red and black jacket as the traveler appeared from the snowy woods. The dog announced Ed's arrival with boisterous barking, and nearly knocked Ed from his snowshoes. The dog danced with excitement at the sight of Ed.

Alice and Bob were pleased to see their good friend. They had their generator working and could make him a hot drink. Alice dug out all sorts of cheeses, cold cuts and breads. They sat in front of a roaring fireplace and caught up on things.

Bob divulged the whereabouts of Meghan. Both Bob and Alice saw a relieved expression come over their friend's face.

Ed explained that his sister and Lyn Grady were unable to fly into Manchester because of the winter storm. He didn't know when they might be able to visit again. Maybe Christmas?

The Finches wondered what Meghan had found out from all her recent research into Jack MacNamara's family. Ed admitted that he would like to divulge some facts he had found. Their family lives had overlapped for decades.

Before long, a bottle of sherry appeared, and some defrosted cookies. More logs were thrown on the fire. Alice offered her guest warm blankets, and she admitted that they planned to stay put unless the electricity didn't come on by Saturday. Then they would find a hotel in Manchester. The roads should be plowed by then. They encouraged Ed to stay the night.

The three sat, silently sipping as daylight slipped away. Max had already found a cushy spot on the end of Ed's down quilt, and was snoring loudly.

"You know, Ed, it was Alice who knew something was going to happen," Bob suddenly said.

"What do you mean?" Ed looked puzzled.

"It was unrelenting in my cards," Alice stated in a matter-of-fact tone.

"So, what did they say?" Ed asked uncharacteristically.

Bob nodded at his wife. The men usually avoided any discussion of Alice's gypsy results.

"The Runes continued to warn about chaos, but at the same time insisting that the situation was on hold and wouldn't resolve itself easily. Just look at this weather! And not just here but in Arizona too," she stated with emphasis. "Certainly, unforeseen forces have created disorder, and won't be settled for a while."

The men were silent and sipped their drinks. The fire spit and snapped as moisture was released from the wood. Max woke and readjusted his wide body.

"It was the Journey card that didn't make any sense to me. But look, Meghan is on the other side of the country now. She is far away from everything."

Alice knew enough not to go too far with her audience, so the conversation turned to other matters. The men discussed sanding the roads and digging out their cars. They wondered when the lake would be frozen enough for snow mobiles, and if the man on the opposite side of the lake would drag out his bob house. But eventually, both men nodded off. Alice added more coverlets and stoked the fire. She carefully added two logs to keep it burning brightly.

Settling down with her own down quilt and woolen blankets, Alice snuggled in. She stared into the fire like humans had done for centuries. She remembered how her grandmother felt that a lit candle helped one to think and to find inner guidance. A candle was always lit during those readings. Fires drew people together, like it was doing there.

"You have a sixth sense, Alice," she had heard her grandmother say. "The cards only assist. You must use this talent with great care."

As Alice gazed into the fireplace on that snowy November night, she felt close to the women who had encouraged her to listen to that inner voice and to help others to do the same.

Christmas was just around the corner. Wasn't a part of that story about the long journey made by the wise men? Didn't they follow a star? Weren't they glad they had?

Closing her eyes, Alice hoped Meghan's journey included a return trip. She hoped her journey brought her favorite neighbor back to Pawtuckaway Lake. She hoped Meghan would follow her heart home.

And she hoped that home was here.

EPILOGUE

Meghan spent two weeks in Arizona. Her neighbors, having already begun the process of rebuilding after the water and winds receded, helped her expedite the repairs on the O'Reilly house.

Larry Bureau had accomplished a lot in the weeks he had remained in Arizona. He served in Afghanistan with the same dedication he applied to all his endeavors. He and his wife hoped to return to Arizona when his mission was finished, and to live there with their children.

The sale of generators skyrocketed in New Hampshire in late 2014. Anyone who was without electricity for more than three days never forgot just how bad hair could look without a hairdryer. Roof rake became a household word, and a four-wheel drive became a staple in many households.

The long-anticipated reunion of the class of 1974 never occurred. There was nowhere to hold it. The snow took weeks to remove, and many of those planning to attend had gathered over pie on the evening of Thanksgiving. They planned a small gathering on a warmer day, and would hold it at Pawtuckaway State Park, hopefully wearing swimsuits.

Ed Shea's handmade birdhouses sold very well in the shops in Wolfeboro, New Hampshire, thanks to his daughter Kate. She managed to sell them at seasonal craft fairs all around Winnipesaukee Lake. She told her father that she saw a man who looked a lot like Sam Norton there accompanied by a very attractive blonde woman. The woman might have been a real estate client, but he really looked like the same man from Hampton

Hills that she had seen in the store where she'd worked the previous summer. Maybe it was someone else.

December would find Meghan returning to Pawtuckaway Lake. She planned to have her family feast at the MacNamara camp for Christmas. She hoped it would be calmer than her failed attempt to hold Thanksgiving there, but she would keep her eyes on the weather, just in case.

Meghan planned to finish the MacNamara family project. Ed Shea planned to coordinate their efforts with his own collection of memorabilia, records and newspaper clippings.

Alice put her Rune cards away for a while. Instead, she spent more time knitting.

Bob and Ed Shea took up ice fishing and had begun to repair some old traps Ed had found in his shed.

As of this writing, it is unknown who might be arriving at Pawtuckaway Lake for Christmas. But that was still weeks away, and there were still so many things to do.

Monica A. Joyal
Author of One Pawtuckaway Summer